The

PLEASURE
OF HIS
COMPANY

Books by Dutch Sheets

From Bethany House Publishers

The
PLEASURE
OF HIS
COMPANY

A JOURNEY TO INTIMATE FRIENDSHIP WITH GOD

DUTCH SHEETS

BETHANY HOUSE PUBLISHERS

a division of Baker Publishing Group
Minneapolis, Minnesota

© 2014 by Dutch Sheets

Published by Bethany House Publishers
11400 Hampshire Avenue South
Bloomington, Minnesota 55438
www.bethanyhouse.com

Bethany House Publishers is a division of
Baker Publishing Group, Grand Rapids, Michigan

Paperback edition published 2015
ISBN 978-0-7642-1333-5

Printed in the United States of America

The Library of Congress has catalogued the hardcover edition as follows:
Sheets, Dutch.
    The pleasure of his company : a journey to intimate friendship
with God / Dutch Sheets.
        pages cm
    Includes bibliographical references.
    Summary: "With biblical insights and personal stories, author
Dutch Sheets takes readers on a 30-day journey to cultivating and
enjoying deeper intimacy with God"—Provided by publisher.
    ISBN 978-0-7642-0948-2 (cloth : alk. paper)
    1. Spirituality—Christianity. 2. Spiritual life—Christianity.
I. Title.
BV4501.3.S531445 2014
248.4—dc23   2013032757

Cover design by Lookout Design, Inc.

15   16   17   18   19   20   7   6   5   4   3   2   1

This book is dedicated
to the memory of my mother,

Mary Lou Doebler,

who taught me how to live with purpose,
love unconditionally, and die with dignity.
She crossed over into the unbroken pleasure
of His company while I was finishing this book.

The great cloud of witnesses
just became greater.

CONTENTS

Contents

1

THE PERSON

PLEASURE.

The word brings to mind many different pictures and thoughts. For many, it might be an exquisite candlelit dinner with someone they love. A relaxing vacation in Hawaii would certainly qualify for most people. To the sports enthusiast, attending a great college football game on a perfect fall day is the ticket. And for the sunbather, there is nothing like a day at the beach. For me, a walk in the woods calms my soul and awakens creativity.

The list could almost be endless, for just as beauty is in the eye of the beholder, pleasure is in the heart of the one experiencing it. For my wife, Ceci, a tomato and mayonnaise sandwich is one of life's simple pleasures (it's a Southern thing). That's an insult to my taste buds.

For Ceci and my daughter Hannah, a pleasurable night of television is an *NCIS* marathon. I think the program is pretty entertaining, but seriously, who in their right mind would choose it over *American Pickers* or *Swamp People*? No doubt about it, tastes vary, and what produces pleasure is highly subjective.

Pleasure is not only determined by the things we do, but also by the company we keep. Personally, I'd rather eat a tomato sandwich with my wife (don't tell her I said that!) than a filet mignon with a few other people I can think of. In fact, I'd take a root canal over an evening with some of them.

A series of effective television commercials features "the most interesting man in the world" as their spokesman. Their descriptions of him are so witty and comical they have inspired enthusiasts to collect and post them on the Internet. Those one-liners describe him as having inside jokes with complete strangers, winning sporting events with his game face alone, and other claims to fame. The quips are witty but, of course, so impossible no one could ever fulfill them.

Though it's an outrageous claim for mere mortals, there actually is an identifiable most interesting person in the world. Not only is He the most interesting individual on earth, but also in heaven. Yahweh is His name. His son, Jesus, is just like Him; so much so that Yahweh actually sent this Son to earth to demonstrate His true nature and characteristics. "If you've seen me, you've seen the Father," Jesus contended. And what did

He reveal to the human family about God's nature? More than this book can relate. Even the gospel writers couldn't present it all. One of Christ's closest followers declared, "There are also many other things which Jesus did, which if they were written in detail, I suppose that even the world itself would not contain the books that would be written" (John 21:25).

Words certainly are inadequate to describe Christ's attributes, abilities, intellect, and accomplishments. He was, and is, breathtaking yet calming, all-powerful but gentle, unsearchably wise though humble, and awe-inspiring while completely approachable. Perfection defines Him, intrigue surrounds Him, and eternity is in Him. He is boundless love, everlasting joy, and the Prince of Peace. Oxymorons are necessary to describe Him, since He is God-man, both human and divine. Incredibly, He's the Ancient of Days, is forever new, and exists in a perpetual now. His nature contradicts every natural law of time, space, and physics. He is the paradox of all paradoxes, and yet in Him there is no duplicity or inconsistency. When a famous leader named Moses asked Him His name, He simply said, "I AM." Whatever you need, I AM is. Words fail.

Young people and old, male and female, rich and poor, moral and immoral—they all found Jesus interesting. He was so magnetic and gentle in His personality that children loved and trusted Him. He was so genuine and caring at heart that immoral women confessed to Him their sordid and painful pasts. On one occasion, a shamed prostitute found deliverance, cleansing, self-worth, and destiny as she bathed Christ's feet with her tears. But He was so overpowering in His masculinity and multifaceted in His gifts that both intellectual businessmen and coarse, tough fishermen left their careers at His simple invitation to "follow Me."

Grown men fell before Jesus in worship, and anointing oil worth thousands of dollars was poured upon His feet. A multitude of men, women, and children—yes, children—sat for *days* at a time listening to Him teach. Families loved having Him in their homes, men liked hiking and camping with Him, and scholars enjoyed picking His brain—when He was only twelve years old! Many more books have been written concerning Him than about any other person, and people sit for hours writing songs about Him.

My meager list barely scratches the surface. Consider the following:

- A fish brought Him a mouthful of money.
- Storms obeyed His commands.
- His spit healed blind eyes and His touch cured leprosy.
- He walked *on* water . . . and *through* walls!
- He turned water into wine and multiplied by thousands a few fish and loaves of bread.
- He raised the dead.
- Insanity fled from Him; demons did, as well.
- Fire goes before Him and consumes His enemies.

- When He died, the sun refused to shine and the earth shook.
- Death, however, couldn't hold Him, and His resurrection was so powerful it spilled over onto other dead people, raising them from the dead!
- His eyes are like fire; His voice is like a waterfall.
- Angels worship Him; rulers cast their crowns at His feet.
- He created everything . . . with just His words.
- He keeps the universe operating in perfect order . . . yep, with just His words.

Consider the magnitude of those last two statements with the following staggering facts. Unless you're a brainiac astronomer, you probably won't be able to grasp them. That's okay. Just get the "wow!" factor.

Begin with our solar system. At the speed of light, 186,000 miles a second, sunlight takes eight minutes to reach the earth. That same light takes five more hours to reach . . . Pluto. After leaving our solar system that same sunlight must travel for four years and four months to reach the next star in the universe. That is a distance of 40 trillion kilometers—mere shoutin' distance in His universe!

The sun resides in the Milky Way Galaxy, which is shaped like a flying saucer, flat and with a bulge in the center. Our sun is roughly three-quarters of the way to the edge of the galaxy. To get a feel for that distance, if our solar system were one inch across, the distance to the center of the Milky Way Galaxy would be 379 miles. Our galaxy contains hundreds of billions of stars.

Yet the Milky Way is but one of roughly one trillion galaxies in the universe. Says astronomer Allan Sandage, "Galaxies are to astronomy what atoms are to physics."

There are twenty galaxies in what is called our local group. The next sort of grouping in the universe is called a supercluster of galaxies. Within our supercluster, the nearest cluster of galaxies, called Virgo, is 50 million light years away. (A light year is the distance light travels in one year. To get a feel for the distance of one light year, if you drove your car at 55 miles per hour, it would take you 12.2 million years to travel one light year.)

Astronomers estimate that the distance across the universe is roughly 40 billion light years and that there are roughly 100 billion trillion stars.[1]

I'm talking about the guy who made all of that . . . with only His words! Truly, there is no one like Jesus.

What if I told you this man requests the pleasure of your company; that this incredible person, the only true and living God, not only loves you, He likes you. He created us, mere humans, because He wanted a family, not distant servants. When Jesus was asked by His disciples to teach them how to pray, His response introduced them to a completely new and radical way of thinking. "Start your prayer by addressing Him as Father," He answered.

When Jesus said this, He forever changed the playing field. He rewrote the rules. Religious leaders were offended, philosophers found it ridiculous, but hungry hearts like yours and mine, looking for our missing soul mate, found it incredibly hope-inspiring.

"You mean that God told us to call Him Dad, not Your Highness or Most Holy One?"

"Yep," Jesus said. "God would prefer that you call Him Dad."

May that forever shape your approach to Yahweh. Father God wants you, not some shallow religious loyalty. The affirmation of your praise and the admiration of your worship blesses Him, not because He needs *them*, but because He needs and wants *you*. The Scriptures tell us He is seeking worshipers, not worship. God isn't insecure, needing our praise in order to feel good about Himself; nor is He proud, needing worship to feed His ego. It is relationship He desires. Intimacy. Family. When we worship, He is captivated by the singer, not the song. Our company is what He longs for. Enlightened worshipers know this. They also know that when they approach Him, He responds; and the pleasure of His company becomes their reward.

Make it yours.

Prayer

Father, I thank You for gifting us with Your most treasured possession—Your one and only Son, Jesus Christ. I am forever grateful and amazed that through relationship with Him, there exists a perfect and limitless revelation of Your heart.

Open the eyes of my heart, Father, to rightly see and intimately know the awe-inspiring person of Your Son, Jesus. Thank You for being forever faithful to Your promise to draw near to me whenever I draw near to You. What a beautiful invitation and blessed assurance.

Jesus, I choose to draw near to You today. I am not satisfied with just knowing of You. I long to know You personally more and more each day. I want to gaze upon Your majestic beauty and rest in the perfection of Your love.

As I embark upon this journey into the depths of who You are, may enjoying the pleasure of Your company become my greatest reward.

(Prayer taken from: John 3:16; Ephesians 1:15–19; 1 Corinthians 2:10; James 4:8; Psalm 27:4; Romans 8:38–39; Genesis 15:1)

2

THE SEEKER

Elevators are convenient . . . and awkward. Who in their right mind likes being in an elevator with people they don't know? The longer the ride, the louder the silence. A few months ago I was trapped in the back of one of these torture chambers in the airport of one of the vacation capitals of the world—Orlando, Florida. Who hasn't heard of Disney World, MGM, and other hot spots there? And based on the lines at these tourist attractions, every person in the world has been there! Consequently, the airport is crowded and hectic. When the elevator stopped at my floor and the door opened, no one moved. After a couple of seconds, thinking no one else was getting off at this level, I spoke up rather urgently from the back, "Excuse me, I need to get off here."

You'd have thought I asked for everyone's phone number! Backs stiffened, eyes glared, and the man closest to the door turned and in a most condescending tone scolded me. "Be patient," he snarled. "I'm just trying to be a *gentleman* and let the ladies off first."

I was tired, and perhaps this had caused me to unintentionally speak louder than I realized. Or maybe my urgency sounded like impatience. Or it could be that the guy in the front of the elevator was a JERK! After we all exited, one of the ladies with him turned to me and, rather snootily, decided to become my counselor: "You need a vacation, sir. We *are* in Orlando; why don't you take a few days off and *chill*." Jerk-ess.

What did I do? Being the gentleman that I am, I took it on the chin and moved on—*with my blood pressure elevated and my inner thoughts explaining to them what idiots they were!* And being the spiritual giant I am, within a few short weeks I had released it and forgiven them. Doesn't take me long!

I hate being misunderstood and misjudged—especially on an elevator! A double whammy of that nature is like being forced to eat broccoli, only to find out as you bite into it that it's spoiled. I don't think God likes being misjudged and misunderstood, either, and He is without doubt the most misunderstood person in existence. Perceived as distant, He is often ignored. Considered judgmental and legalistic, He is thought by some to be intimidating and one to steer clear of. And mistakenly thought of by His children as one who likes to hear how great He is, He is praised.

Don't misunderstand. Praising God is obviously good and appropriate. It's our reason for doing so that needs some serious tweaking. He isn't narcissistic, needing to be told how wonderful He is in order to satisfy an inflated ego, and He isn't insecure, needing to be reassured that He really is awesome. He doesn't show off—praise does not stimulate some macho corner of His heart, motivating Him to action in order to demonstrate His power. And He can't be bought—our worship doesn't cause Him to "reward" us with His presence simply because we made Him feel so good. The body of Christ has lots of strange ideas about praise and worship. Frankly, God neither *needs* nor *wants* worship.

He is, however, seeking *worshipers*.

The difference is huge—immeasurably so. *We ARE the worship*. God longs for the singer, not the song. Our heart as a worshiper is what makes our *singing* worship, not the words and music. He'd rather have a love-filled glance from your eyes than a song parroted from your lips.

When my kids were young and anxiously waited for Daddy to come home from work, they didn't meet me at the door with a song. They jumped into my arms and gave me a big hug.

When God created us, He made kids, not a choir; family members, not church members. He's into love, not liturgy.

Too often we make worship simply a segment of a service, rather than a time to become intimate with Jesus. And in our services the speaker is usually allotted more time than worship of Jesus is. I often look over the crowd to see how many people seem truly focused on the words they're singing and the One they're supposedly singing to. Obviously, I can't judge the hearts of people. But if I requested a heart-to-heart conversation with my wife, then pulled out a script and timer, she wouldn't consider it "heart-to-heart." And if I displayed the mannerisms and body language to her that many "worshipers" in our services display, she would feel anything but honored and appreciated. Actually, she would probably feel *dishonored*. And who could blame her—she would know it was a token conversation, not a heartfelt exchange.

I don't mean to be critical. Actually, I don't believe the problem with most believers' worship is hypocrisy or insincerity. I think the majority is honestly trying to honor God by giving Him His dues and fulfilling their obligation to Him as the Creator. I doubt if most of them understand, or have even heard, that God is a lover as well as a Lord. And it wasn't His *lording* nature that prompted Him to create us—He could have made a few billions more angels had that been His desire. It was His *loving* nature. God is a Father at heart.

Jesus, who came to earth to show us what God is truly like, gave a great glimpse of the Father's loving heart through an encounter with a rather loose-living woman. Looking for love in all the wrong places, this five-time divorced, currently shacked-up societal outcast was about to meet a man who wanted her heart, not her body.

Left alone with her at a well while His disciples went looking for food, Jesus first shocked this woman by breaking Jewish protocol and engaging her in conversation. Based on the ensuing dialogue, it seems obvious that He knew her lifestyle from the moment He saw her. It also seems obvious He intended to change it. "Go, call your husband and come here," He said to her.

"I have no husband," the woman answered Him.

Then, in His inimitable, supernatural way, Jesus cut to the chase. "You have correctly said, 'I have no husband'; for you have had five husbands, and the one whom you now have is not your husband; this you have said truly" (John 4:16–18). The Lord wasn't saying this to condemn the woman but to get her attention and begin to reveal who He actually was. He had seen something more than lust for sensual pleasure when He looked into this woman's soul; He saw a thirsty heart and potential worshiper.

Knowing He would first have to lead her out of the blinding fog of non-relational religion and past the stumbling block of racial division, Jesus dodged her question about *where* she should worship and went straight to *how*:

> Jesus said to her, "Woman, believe Me, an hour is coming when neither in this mountain nor in Jerusalem

will you worship the Father. You worship what you do not know; we worship what we know, for salvation is from the Jews. But an hour is coming, and now is, when the true worshipers will worship the Father in spirit and truth; for such people the Father seeks to be His worshipers. God is spirit, and those who worship Him must worship in spirit and truth."

John 4:21–24

Jesus had already told this woman He knew her life-style, and His actions prove He wasn't condemning her. He had assured her He could satisfy her thirsty heart by placing a well of salvation in her. Now He was going to the heart of the matter: worship. He shifted the concept of worship from the *place* to the *person*, which was a radical paradigm shift in her day. I'm sure she had never thought about this, and certainly not that God was actually *seeking* worshipers. "He'd like you to be one" was the obvious invitation.

She was hooked. That God might actually be seeking her companionship was beyond this woman's wildest dreams. How could He possibly want her? But He did. In one moment her shame was broken and joy filled her heart. It feels good to be wanted for the right reasons. This new worshiper was so excited, she ran and told the men of her village about Jesus, and they, too, ended up believing on Him. (I don't think the women talked to her!) Ultimately, the entire community believed on Him.

Jesus was too excited to eat!

When the disciples returned, they were amazed that He was speaking to this immoral woman. Jesus was impervious to their shock, however, and completely unconcerned about His reputation. His excitement about transforming lives and finding true worshipers was far greater than any concern over His reputation. On one occasion, He actually allowed a prostitute to enter a person's home and, while they ate, bathe His feet with her tears. Awkward! But not to Him; He was on a search for true worshipers, and their pasts weren't an issue with Him, only their hearts.

Christ is still seeking true worshipers today. If the God you've been introduced to is distant, uncaring, stoic, or enamored with Himself, you've been duped. The real God is passionate, caring, a lover of people, and a seeker of companionship—yours. While others seek His help, why don't you seek His heart? Make His day by giving Him the pleasure of some company.

Prayer

Thank You, Father, for sending to us a Savior who shattered false ideologies regarding Your nature by demonstrating what You are truly like and showing us the way to Your heart.

Good Shepherd, I am forever grateful to You for going out in search of this one lost sheep. Your eyes never tire of looking into the darkest of places to passionately seek and satisfy souls who thirst for true love.

I stand amazed at the reality that You—the Creator of the Universe—would lovingly long for my companionship. You are the only god who wants my heart more than my worship. Such love! What a good Father and Friend You are.

Jesus, I too desire relationship with You. Rather than seek Your help today, I choose to seek Your beautiful heart. I want to respond to the love that You extended to me first. It would be my great pleasure to keep You company and satisfy the longings of Your heart.

(Prayer taken from: John 14:8–11; John 10:11; Luke 19:10; 2 Chronicles 16:9; John 4:23; 1 John 4:19)

3

THE DISCOVERY

In the last chapter we saw God as a seeker, always searching for those who have hearts that want to know Him. The reciprocal must be true, as well. In any true relationship there can only be fulfillment if the pursuit is both ways. When it is, the seeking becomes an exciting adventure and leads to the joy of discovery.

Judging by kids, there's something born into our hearts that makes us enjoy the pursuit. Whether it's a treasure hunt, an Easter egg hunt, or hide-and-seek, the buildup of anticipation and expectation adds a sense of mystique to the process and the search becomes an adventure.

I started playing hide-and-seek indoors with my daughters, Sarah and Hannah, when they were very young. They weren't very good at it. I could always find places to hide—under a blanket, in a closet, under a table. Wanting them to enjoy the game, however, I would make small noises to reveal my hiding place. They would fling open the door or jerk back the blanket and shriek for joy as I acted bummed out because they had found me. They knew, of course, I wasn't really upset, just having fun. I actually loved it when they found me.

God plays hide-and-seek with His kids, as well. And He, too, loves it when we find Him. "If you seek Him, He will let you find Him," said Azariah, an Old Testament prophet, to Israel (2 Chronicles 15:2). The people listened to Azariah and sought the Lord, and, just as God promised, He allowed them to find Him:

> All Judah rejoiced concerning the oath, for they had sworn with their whole heart and had sought Him earnestly, and He let them find Him. So the Lord gave them rest on every side.
>
> 2 Chronicles 15:15

When we "discover" God, as He allowed Israel to do, we find far more than just the *pleasure* of His company, as wonderful as that is. We also find our *purpose*. Jeremiah spoke of finding both God and purpose in the following verses:

> "For I know the plans that I have for you," declares the Lord, "plans for welfare and not for calamity to give you a future and a hope. Then you will call upon Me and come and pray to Me, and I will listen to you.

You will seek Me and find Me when you search for Me
with all your heart."

Jeremiah 29:11–13

The Hebrew word translated "future" in this passage
is *achariyth*. It also means "destiny." "When you search
for Me with all your heart," the Lord was assuring them,
"not only will I let you find Me, I'll also allow you to
discover My plans and purposes for you. Pleasure and
purpose are both found in My company."

As with any created thing, our purpose can only be
found in the heart and mind of our Creator. When we
seek Him, we are actually pursuing destiny; find one,
you've found the other. William Wilberforce, the great
English statesman who was used by God to end slavery
in the British Empire, is a great example. Wilberforce
sought God, found Him, and in so doing also discovered
his destiny as a reformer. In the movie chronicling his
life, *Amazing Grace*, there is a scene in which Wilberforce's butler stumbles upon him praying and meditating. This was unusual, so the butler asks Wilberforce
if he has found God. "I think He found me," is the
poignant response.

When the seeking starts, sometimes it's hard to know
who finds whom! Did we find God or did He find us?
Actually, it's both. He initiates the process by pursuing
us; we respond by returning His love. "We love, because
He first loved us" (1 John 4:19). This pattern occurred
several years ago in my life in a most dramatic way.

It was 1973, and I was attending college, traveling fast but going nowhere. I had been running from God for two years, serving the gods of alcohol, drugs, and rock 'n' roll. Though I had been raised in church (Dad was an evangelist and then a pastor) and had surrendered my life to Christ at a young age, at seventeen I began to rebel. The rebellion started when my dad had an affair with his secretary, left our family, and married her.

As you can imagine, our lives were shattered. Mom found a job in a meat market, my brother and I found part-time jobs, and somehow we survived. At least physically. We didn't fare so well emotionally and spiritually. My brother and I rebelled, turning away from God and everything associated with Him. My younger sister was also emotionally devastated; obviously, so was my mom. Deep in my heart I knew this wasn't God's fault, but nonetheless I was angry at Him. The pain was so strong and my confusion so great that I simply couldn't cope with it. And I certainly couldn't understand it. Perhaps the lowest point in my life was the day when, as a seventeen-year-old, I held my mother in my arms and listened to her sob and tell me she no longer wanted to live. At that moment, I became a very bitter and hate-filled young man.

God was very patient with me. He knew my rebellion was caused by my pain. He allowed me to run, loved me through my pain-filled responses, and didn't take them personally. Two years later, at a bar named The Boars Head—aptly so, since I was a prodigal and this was my pigpen—while I was listening to a rock band and stoned out of my mind, He found me.

"What are you doing here?" He asked. The Lord's voice was so clear it may as well have been audible. The question wasn't a rebuke but rather a sincere prompting of my heart. "You know this is not who you are," He continued, "and you'll never find the fulfillment and peace you're looking for through this lifestyle."

Shocked and amazed that God would pursue me into a place like this, my first response was, "What are *You* doing here?!"

"I've come for you."

Instantly sober, I went outside to walk and think for a while. The Lord and I had several more conversations over the next couple of months, until I was finally healed enough to respond to His seeking. I sought Him back . . . and He let me find Him. Like the prodigal returning to his father's embrace, I walked back into the loving embrace of Papa God. When I did, I found more than pleasure; I discovered purpose.

Realizing that the field of study I was pursuing was not what I was created to do, I withdrew from college. As he had Wilberforce, the Lord had found me and was now awakening passions and desires from deep within. Just as I had done with my girls, He started making small "noises," and I experienced the excitement of discovery.

I entered into a passionate pursuit of God, became active in a good local church, and connected with other hungry seekers. I also began going on short-term missions trips, serving missionaries and the poor in Guatemala. Eventually realizing I wanted to serve God in full-time ministry, I decided to attend Christ For The Nations Institute in Dallas, Texas. There I discovered God—over and over—and eventually I discovered my wife, to whom I've been married for thirty-five wonderful years. It has been a great journey.

When the Lord pursued me and helped me find Him, my destiny truly was launched. Finding Him is finding the source of everything good. Out of the deep resources of His nature, all good things flow. He and I have been pursuing each other now for thirty-nine years. I have found Him in forests, on mountains, at the edge of streams, riding in my truck, in front of fireplaces, and, yes, in worship services. The discoveries require time and effort, of course—any worthwhile relationship does—but each time I rediscover Him I realize again that He is life's treasure.

I'll bet if you listen closely right now, you'll find that He's making some noises. Why don't you go find Him.

Prayer

Father, I thank You for relentlessly pursuing me with Your unconditional love and making a way for me to find You through the life of Your glorious Son.

I respond to Your love-driven seeking today and set myself upon a steadfast pursuit of Your heart. Jesus, You are the source of both pleasure and purpose—dreams realized through hearts set aflame. Truly, You are the fountain of every good thing.

Thank You for revealing and releasing me into my destiny as I draw near to know the depths of Your heart. May Your goodness continually lead me to discover the amazing adventures, exquisite joys, and profound fulfillment that lie within the pleasure of Your company.

(Prayer taken from: John 14:6–11; 1 John 4:19; Isaiah 55:6; Deuteronomy 4:29; 2 Chronicles 15:15; Psalm 34:8; Psalm 36:6; Jeremiah 29:11–13; Jeremiah 33:3; Hebrews 11:6)

4

THE DANCE

I'm not a great dancer. Okay, I'm not even an average dancer. Fine, I can't dance at all. When I was in high school, there was a popular dance called the Funky Chicken. I think my version of this controlled flopping was probably the closest I've ever come to performing a dance properly. I actually thought I was pretty good at it until my friends tagged my version the Flopping Chicken. Mom walked in on me practicing once and freaked out. "Are you okay?" she screamed, thinking I was having a seizure.

"Yeah, I'm good," I assured her. "Just doing the Funky Chicken."

"Get him off sugar," Dad murmured from across the room, "before he breaks something."

"Looks like he's being stung by a swarm of bees," joked my brother.

A few years back, my wife, Ceci, talked me into taking some private ballroom dancing lessons. I resisted at first, knowing this wouldn't end well, but it became clear it was important to her. So against all wisdom, I succumbed.

You've probably heard the expression, but have you ever really seen a drunken sailor? My dogs actually ran outside—wouldn't come close to me for days. "Maybe we should just take walks together," Ceci suggested.

"Yeah," I said, "unless they bring back the Funky Chicken."

Dancing, for those who are fortunate enough to have the right genes, is considered great fun. It is, in fact, associated with joy. Who hasn't heard the phrase "dancing for joy"? When we are sad we tend to become more inactive, but when we're joyful or celebrating we jump, dance, and twirl around.

So does God.

No, I'm not kidding. He dances. There is a little-known verse in the Old Testament that gives a wonderful description of God's dancing heart toward His kids: "The Lord your God is in your midst, a victorious warrior. He will exult over you with joy, He will be quiet in His love, He will rejoice over you with shouts of joy" (Zephaniah 3:17). The last phrase of this verse in the KJV reads, "He will joy over thee with singing." In Hebrew, the language in which the Old Testament was written, the word translated "rejoice" (NASB) and "joy" (KJV) is the Hebrew word *guwl*, which literally means "to spin around under the influence of any violent emotion." That's what I said—He dances.

Hebrew is a pictorial language; a word paints a picture or creates an image. With this word picture *guwl* presents—spinning around emotionally—it's easy to see why it is translated into English words like *joy*, *rejoice*, *glad*, and *delight*. But really, do these translations do justice to this awesome little word? No way.

I experienced joy last weekend when through my status as an Executive Platinum flyer with American Airlines, I was upgraded to first class. I actually rejoiced, sending a text to Ceci that read, "Awesome! Upgraded!" But I didn't jump up in the terminal and dance around. I also experienced joy when the Baltimore Ravens football team beat the New England Patriots a few weeks back. (It's not that I'm a Ravens fan; I just don't like the Patriots.) But on neither of these occasions did I *guwl*.

However, when my favorite football team, the Denver Broncos, won the Super Bowl a few years back, I *guwl*-ed. Losing all dignity, I jumped, screamed, and spun around, shaking my fists in the air. I high-fived everyone around me, whether I knew them or not. *Guwl*-ing brings people together! The day I'm writing this chapter happens to be New Year's Eve. People will be *guwl*-ing all over the world tonight with individuals they don't even know.

But really, Dutch, are you saying God acts this way over His kids? Absolutely. In the great story of the prodigal son (Luke 15:11–32), the prodigal's father depicts our heavenly Father. When the wayward son returns home, his father was so excited he threw a party accompanied with music, dancing, and great rejoicing. I can't prove it, but I know who was leading the dance. Dad! The guy who ran to meet his returning son, butchered the fattened calf, and threw the party. One of my favorite lexicons says the word *rejoice* in this passage may be related to a different Hebrew word that describes a young sheep or lamb skipping and frisking for joy. The same word is used to describe how angels in heaven act when a person comes to Christ (Luke 15:10). There's a new description of heaven for most of us—a happy, playful, skipping God with His happy, frolicking angels!

Some will think I'm insulting God's dignity by ascribing to Him human emotion and celebrative actions. Let me assure you that this is not my intention. I don't for a moment believe He acts like us—I believe we act like Him! We were created in God's image and likeness. That means we have emotions because He has emotions: We love because He loves, laugh because He laughs, cry because He cries, and dance because He dances. If your concept of Him is a distant, stoic, and boring entity that sounds like Cecil B. DeMille's rendition of Jehovah in the movie *The Ten Commandments*, think again. God is fun, cool, "real," and will be the life of heaven's party.

You've probably read the popular "Footprints" poem, which depicts the Lord carrying us through difficult seasons of life. I like the following version even better.

A woman had a dream in which her life with Jesus was pictured by footprints in the sand.

For much of the way, the Lord's footprints went along steadily, consistently, rarely varying in the pace. Her prints, however, were in a disorganized stream of zigzags, starts, stops, turnarounds, circles, departures, and returns. For a long while they seemed to go like this. But gradually, her footprints came in line with the Lord's, eventually paralleling His consistently. She and Jesus were walking as true friends.

This seemed perfect, but then an interesting thing happened; her footprints that once etched the sand next to the Master's were now walking precisely in His steps. Inside His large footprints were the smaller prints, safely enclosed. She and Jesus were becoming one; this went on for many miles.

But gradually she noticed another change. The footprints inside the larger footprints seemed to grow bigger. Eventually they disappeared altogether. There was only one set of footprints; they had become one. Again, this went on for a long time.

Then something awful happened. The second set of footprints was back. This time it seemed even worse than at the beginning. Zigzags all over the place . . . stop, start . . . deep gashes in the sand . . . a veritable mess of prints. She was amazed and shocked. But this was the end of her dream.

The lady went to the Lord in prayer, seeking to understand: "Lord, I understand the first scene with the zigzags, fits, starts, and so on. I was a new Christian, just learning. But You walked on and helped me learn to walk with You."

"That is correct," replied the Lord.

"Then, when the smaller footprints were inside of Yours, I was actually learning to walk in Your steps. I followed You very closely."

"Very good. You have understood everything so far."

"Then the smaller footprints grew and eventually filled in Yours. I suppose that I was actually growing so much that I was becoming more like You in every way."

"Precisely."

"But this is my question, Lord. The footprints went back to two, and this time it was more chaotic than at the first. Was there a regression in my life?"

The Lord smiles, then laughs. "You didn't know?" He says. "That was when we danced."[1]

That's what I'm talking about!

I'm fully aware that the super-religious crowd won't approve of my fun-loving God. This depiction of Him will be considered irreverent by them, perhaps even heretical. If you really want to know what they believe about God's personality, go to one of their worship services. But—and forgive me for being so blunt—you might want to drink an espresso on the way. Frankly, I think even God gets bored with many of their church services. Trust me, the God of Scripture isn't starchy and religious.

Our worship gatherings should be celebrations where we join hands with Papa God and have a little fun frisking, leaping, and dancing. (Just don't do the Funky Chicken.) *Shabath*, the Hebrew word for sabbath, means not only "to stop or cease from work" but also "to celebrate." In much the same way we celebrate certain days—holidays, for example—by resting from work, this is the concept of *shabath*. On the seventh day, God stopped working and celebrated! He was so excited about having a family He decided it would be commemorated with a "rest and celebration day." That puts a new twist on taking a sabbath. Every seventh day we should all rest and celebrate our membership in God's family with joy and great rejoicing. If we would do so, the gospel we preach would be a lot more appealing.

Abandon your concept of a passionless God. Reject all religious stereotyping of Him. Let your heavenly Father be real, relevant, and relational. Only then will you begin to experience the pleasure of His company.

Look up. . . . I think He's asking for this dance.

Prayer

Heavenly Father, I thank You for loving us so intensely that You would choose to dwell in our midst. What a staggering revelation is Your love expressed in Emmanuel—Your Savior Son, the Word made flesh, both man and God with us.

Jesus, my beloved Bridegroom, I am amazed at Your passionate love toward me, leaping and skipping at the mere thought of encountering my heart. Then You rejoice over me with sweet love songs and with shouts of exuberant jubilee. You are the Almighty God who dances zealously over me. Astounding!

I am overjoyed with gratitude to have as Lord over my life a fun-loving God who is real, relevant, and relational. I want to learn to receive the full expression of Your love.

Father, may my heart's response to Your passionate love be ever-increasingly undignified. Like David, I want to dance unashamedly for You. Open my ears to hear the sounds of heaven and cease from my labors long enough to freely bask in the celebrations of Your love. Sweet Daddy, shall we dance?

(Prayer taken from: Ezekiel 48:35; Isaiah 7:14; Matthew 1:23; Zephaniah 3:17; Psalm 32:7; Song of Solomon 2:8; Luke 15:11–32; 2 Samuel 6:14, 20–22)

5

The Search

I have many great memories of times with the three ladies in my life: Ceci, my wife; my older daughter, Sarah; and Hannah, my younger. The pleasure of their company has always been special to me.

Of the thousands of memorable days I've spent with Ceci, one exciting excursion on a beautiful Saturday in the spring of '77 stands out. We had gone to picturesque White Rock Lake in Dallas, Texas, where we enjoyed a wonderful picnic. Ceci cooked some of her great fried chicken and prepared some potato salad for the occasion. After eating, we sat on a blanket not far from the lake—the setting was absolutely perfect—and enjoyed some pleasant conversation. She had brought along her guitar, and we enjoyed singing a few worship songs; the presence of the Holy Spirit was sweet. In this beautiful setting, on this beautiful day, totally mesmerized by this beautiful lady, I asked her to marry me. Finding me irresistible, she said yes.

Of the many memories made with Sarah, her wedding is certainly one of the preeminent. I recall the pride and satisfaction I felt when she and I danced at her reception. Actually, as you might have guessed from reading the last chapter, shifting my weight from one foot to the other while holding her hand and shoulder was about as creative as the dancing got. But that didn't matter. The important part was looking into her eyes, telling her how beautiful she was and how proud her mother and I were. I spent a fortune that day. "Thank you, Daddy," was all the return I needed.

In regards to Hannah, I love to recall the camping trip she and I embarked on several years ago. We found a beautiful spot on a stream in Colorado, and spent the weekend enjoying nature and nature's God. As we drove through Rocky Mountain National Park one morning, a park with views that rival anything in the world, we were also listening to beautiful worship songs she and I love. I'll never forget the tears that flowed down Hannah's cheeks at one point as she marveled at God's majesty and reveled in His love. Happy tears. Peaceful tears. "I'm in love with God and He's in love with me" tears.

What was it that made those days so memorable for me? With Ceci, was it a lake, a guitar, a blanket, and some good food? Of course not; those were simply adornments that created helpful ambiance. With Sarah, was it the uniqueness and joy of a celebrative wedding atmosphere? Not really. I've been to many weddings that hold no such memories for me. With Hannah, was it the beauty and majesty of the Colorado Rockies? As amazing as they are, and as much as they "garnished" the day, it wasn't the mountains.

It was the company.

Sparkling eyes, smiles, embraces, laughter, happy tears, and hearts I connected with at a deep level—these made the memories special. It was the lady, not the lake; the girl I was dancing with, not the dance; the passenger, not the drive. Whom you're with matters most in life.

I've made some great memories with God, just as I have with my three ladies. He and I have laughed and cried together; and yes, we've danced a time or two. We have sat, walked, ridden, and bicycled in each other's company. I've crawled up in His lap and napped, sang Him songs, and watched a few movies with Him. He is more than a "being" to me. He's a companion. Not making His acquaintance would have been life's greatest injustice.

Does He feel the same way about us? Of course He does. He loves being with us. Consider the following invitation: "Behold, I stand at the door, and knock: if any man hear my voice, and open the door, I will come in to him, and will sup with him, and he with me" (Revelation 3:20 KJV). The Almighty, the Creator, the Everlasting God of heaven and earth requests the pleasure of your company tonight for dinner.

What a thought!

Do you, like me, find it interesting that He *knocks* on the door? I suppose God could simply knock it down. Or just walk through it! But that would be intrusion, and God doesn't want to intrude into your space; He wants to be invited in. Like anyone, He wants to be celebrated, not tolerated.

The word *sup* in this verse is not a generic word that refers to eating. This is the word in biblical times for the main evening meal. The Jewish new day began in the evening, at sunset. At this evening meal, the family would gather to discuss the day's events, and the new day would begin and be planned. Jesus is saying to us in this verse, "Let me into your world. Let's dine, fellowship, and plan the day."

I have a friend who used to set a literal table for himself and the Lord every Friday night. He made it as elaborate as possible with fine china, candles, nice silverware—the works. It was a weekly, formal date with the Lord. Convinced the Father was present, he spoke to Him throughout his meal. And he listened. Why did he take such a radical step? To aid himself in becoming consciously aware that the Lord was always present, and to forever seal in his mind and heart that He wanted to sup with him. It was a simple but powerful visual aid.

Many would think him silly, some would even believe he was in need of psychiatric help, but this drastic measure worked for my friend. He learned to commune with the Lord as a real person and on a personal level. He also learned to hear and discern God's voice. This ability is not a gift, but rather a learned art. When you take the time to wait and listen, you learn to allow God into your thinking. His thoughts become yours. In this verse, the Lord said, "If any man hear my voice . . ." The obvious insinuation is that *our* actions, not His, will determine whether or not we hear from Him. Again, sensitivity is learned and developed. Like the frequencies on a radio, our minds and hearts must tune in.

One of my employees a few years back related the following humorous episode about listening.

> While my sister-in-law was busy in the kitchen preparing dinner and planning for various family and church activities, her young daughter continued to talk to her about many different important things in her life, to which her mother would periodically respond, "Uh-huh." Finally, wanting to do something to make this more of a two-sided conversation, the little girl tugged on her mother's arm to get her full attention. Once she knew her mother was really listening, she said, "Mom, why don't you talk for a while now, and I'll say 'Uh-huh.'"[1]

I can't help but wonder how often God is knocking and calling, only to find us so busy we really aren't listening. He will never treat us this way. You'll never find Him so busy with others or so distracted running the universe that He feigns attentiveness to you, mumbling "uh-huh" while actually thinking about something else.

He has plenty of undistracted time for you, and He wants some in return.

The Scriptures suggest that God is searching for this kind of relationship. From the moment we were separated from Him by Adam's sin, He began the search. "Where are you?" He called to Adam and Eve as they hid from Him (Genesis 3:9). We're told that His eyes "move to and fro" throughout the earth looking for those whose hearts are fully His (2 Chronicles 16:9).

One of my favorite Bible stories as a young kid was about a man named Zaccheus. He was a tax collector and had become wealthy, most likely by defrauding people, charging them more than they actually owed. Somehow this man had become enamored with Jesus, so much so that he climbed a tree to get a good look at Him as He passed through his village. Jesus wanted Zaccheus to get more than a look, however; He invited Himself over for dinner! "Zaccheus, hurry and come down, for today I must stay at your house" (Luke 19:5).

Jesus knocked and Zaccheus opened. The visit was obviously impactful. It always is when Jesus comes over for dinner. "Lord, half of my possessions I'll give to the poor," he promised before the meeting ended, "and if I have defrauded anyone of anything, I will give back four times as much" (Luke 19:8).

When challenged as to why He would be the guest of a man who was a "sinner," Jesus merely referenced His searching heart. "For the Son of Man has come to *seek* and to save that which was lost," (v. 10, italics mine).

He simply has an insatiable desire to eat and fellowship with friends and family.

Jesus was on a mission then; He's on the same mission now. He wants to make some memories with you. The next time He knocks, open the door. Make your house one of the regular stops for His searching eyes.

Prayer

Father, I am so grateful for the invitation to intimacy that at every moment remains extended unto me. Jesus, as one courting the bride whom He adores, You never stop seeking to ravish my heart.

Oh, that my heart would stay awake to always receive the kind visitations of my Beloved. Let no distraction, hesitation, or slumbering soul be found within me. May my heart always remain an open door to You, Jesus, as I seek to mature in the art of discerning Your knock and Your voice. Sensitize me more and more to Your promptings with every response to Your love.

As Your eyes search this world for a surrendered heart with which to commune, let Your gaze rest upon me. You are welcomed to sit at the supper table of my soul to dine and dialogue together. I need and want You present in the details of my every day. I would love to receive the pleasure of Your company today.

(Prayer taken from: Genesis 3:9; Revelation 3:20; Luke 19:10; Song of Solomon 4:9; 5; 2 Chronicles 16:9)

6

THE PRIORITY

Firsts" can be good or bad. First place is usually good, as are first class and first rate. First degree is usually bad, as is the need for first aid, and the first half and first baseman can be either. While thinking about this chapter, I recalled several of my firsts and a one- or two-word thought concerning them. Here are ten:

- First major-league baseball game (awe)
- First day of school (intimidated)
- First bike (fast)
- First car (junk)
- First time seeing color TV (mesmerized)
- First date with Ceci (priceless)
- First time seeing both daughters (love)
- First dirty diaper change (nausea)

- First cell phone (heavy)
- First sermon (nice try)

Compiling a few of my firsts was fun. Some were extremely important, others only memorable. The same would be true if you compiled a list. There is one first, however, that is essential and that all of us must have in common. Jesus referred to it as our "first love." When writing to the Ephesian church He said, "But I have this against you, that you have left your first love" (Revelation 2:4).

The Greek word translated "first" in this passage is *protos*, meaning "foremost in time, place, order, or importance." Since it would be illogical to assume Christ had been the first person each of them had loved, it seems reasonable to conclude He was using the word in the sense of importance. "You have abandoned the love that should be your number one priority," was His obvious meaning.

The root word for *protos* is *pro*, meaning "superior to" or "in front of," and yes, it is where we get our word *professional*, or its shortened form, *pro*. A professional is one who is superior to others in a particular field. I'm a golfer; Phil Mickelson is, as well. But there's a big difference between us: He's a pro, I'm an amateur. Watching each of us swing a golf club once would leave no doubt as to the difference.

Shopping is another activity performed by both pros and amateurs. I shop once in a while—when God is punishing me for speeding or some other sin. I'm an amateur shopper, and have no desire to ever be anything but an amateur. Ceci, on the other hand, is a pro. And as is fitting, she loves it. We have reached the glorious state in our marriage wherein she no longer makes me shop for her birthday or Christmas presents. Oh, I grab a few stocking stuffers and surprise her once in a while with a really cool present like a toaster or lamp, but for the most part she does all the shopping. The reason? She'd rather have what she likes most and fits her the best. So I buy her gift cards—really neat ones with cool pictures—purchased from the appropriate stores. Then we both do what we do best: I watch football and she shops. Life is good.

Placing the literal definitions of *pro* and *protos* into the context of Revelation 2:4 makes clear what Jesus was saying: Relationship with Him should be "in front of" or "superior to" all others. He wants to be our "priority" love. He told us elsewhere that loving Him is the first and foremost of all the other commandments (Matthew 22:38).

This begs the question of why—why does God demand to be first? Is He conceited or egocentric, demanding that we make Him the center of attention? Or is God insecure and in need of our affirmation? The answer to both of these questions, of course, is a resounding no. The Lord is self-confident and self-assured, and yet this is filtered through the utmost humility. He has neither pride nor insecurity issues. Why, then, does He want to be number one?

The reason God must be first in our lives is profound in both its simplicity and importance: *The very purpose for the creation of humans was relationship with God.* We were formed to be one in spirit with Him, joined together like a husband and wife. First Corinthians 6:17 says, "But the one who joins himself to the Lord is one spirit with Him." Our union with Him completes us. There is a place in the heart of every human that God made only for Himself. Period. If we don't get this right, life will be out of rhythm; the pieces won't fit. Nothing else can fill this void, including other people, money, pleasure, or accomplishments. And certainly not religion. We weren't created to connect with a system but a person.

God understands this, of course, and for our benefit reminds us of His love for us and of our need for Him. Our connection with Him affects everything, including all other relationships. God is love, and knowing Him awakens love in us, both for Him and for others (1 John 4:7–8). The more we connect with Him and His love-nature, the better lovers we'll be of our families, friends, and fellow humans. In fact, in the above verse the Lord tells us the person who doesn't love doesn't know Him. Knowing and loving God is the launch point for all of life. If the first thing isn't first, everything else is out of order.

The context of the warning in Revelation 2:4 alludes to this. In the prior verses, Christ gave the Ephesians an evaluation any Christian would be thrilled to have. Read it carefully:

> I know your deeds and your toil and perseverance, and that you cannot endure evil men, and you put to the test those who call themselves apostles, and they are not, and you found them to be false; and you have perseverance and have endured for My name's sake, and have not grown weary.

Revelation 2:2–4

What believer wouldn't be excited to hear this praise? Most of us couldn't score high in all of these areas. Yet Christ makes it clear that these accomplishments are not the heart of the matter. A good performance can't take the place of intimacy with Him. If this is allowed to occur, our good works will devolve into empty religion every time, *satisfying neither God nor us*. Our performance must flow out from relationship with Him, never replace or be equated to it.

It is also important to understand that our first, or priority, love is not based on emotions or feelings. It would be unrealistic to think we can maintain the same level of emotional excitement that typically occurs when we first meet Christ. Such a sustained emotional high is not a reasonable expectation in any relationship, whether that be with our spouse, a friend, or the Lord. Emotions are fickle, coming and going based on our moods and circumstances. Love, however, is not an emotion; it is a choice, as are priorities. Love is chosen, not "fallen" in and out of. I don't always "feel" my love for my wife and daughters, but I always love them. They are, and will remain, my highest earthly priorities.

Marriages built on feelings become divorces; parenting based on emotions results in fatherless and motherless children; and Christians who base their pursuit of God on feelings and emotions become lukewarm, passionless, and indifferent. They may not walk away from their faith, but they will always leave their first love. How sad this is, and so avoidable.

David, the great psalmist and king of Israel, demonstrated the danger of losing first love. Known as being one of the most passionate God-seekers ever, David loved being with Him. "O Lord, I love the habitation of Your house and the place where Your glory dwells," he told the Lord (Psalm 26:8). There came a time, however, when compromise entered David's life and other passions began to outweigh His passion for God. Success can be a thief, robbing us of the zeal that produced it, and this happened with David. It was his zealous heart after God that gained David the throne, not his gifts or good looks (see 1 Samuel 16:7). But success tempered this zeal, and eventually the pleasures of the palace replaced the pleasure of God's company.

When David's compromise became great enough, temptation was presented. It always happens this way. Jesus warned us that temptation would come, not at haphazard and random moments, but at *kairos* times (Luke 8:13). *Kairos* means "strategic or opportune time; the right time." Satan and his demons watch and wait for the perfect time to strike. They've been practicing for six thousand years and know their craft well. The tempter knows that when the shield of our love commitment is lowered, the potential for compromise rises.

From his palace roof, David saw a beautiful lady bathing. Having lost the sustaining power of his first-love relationship with God, Bathsheba entered his life. His sin resulted in her becoming pregnant, which led him to cause the death of her righteous husband, Uriah, so he could marry her. How could David, a man after God's heart, fall to such depravity? One step at a time, beginning with the loss of his first love. He eventually made it back, but it was a long and painful process involving great heartache and loss.

If Christ is currently number one in your life and you're enjoying the pleasure of His company, treasure it. Let nothing come between the two of you. But if you, like David, or the church of Ephesus, have allowed other things to take priority over your relationship with Him, reprioritize. Make Him *protos* again—superior to all else. And if you have never yet discovered Christ as your first love soul mate—well, get ready to find out why you exist.

Amazing joys await you.

Prayer

Father, You are holy, incomparable, and superior in every way. Your Name, Jesus, is above every other name. You hold the place of highest honor and all else must bow at Your feet.

You are the everlasting Creator-King, yet You choose to commune with me. Jesus, You are worthy of my diligent devotion. You are worthy of my unashamed love.

Holy Spirit, search my heart and show me where I've failed to ascribe to God the highest place. Reveal to me the ways in which I have compromised my commitment to You, forsaking my first love. Thank You for tenderly drawing my wayward heart back to the priority of loving You and receiving Your love.

Jesus, I truly want to live my life out of the first commandment; loving You first and fully, and from there, sharing Your love with the world. My heart's desire is that in all things You would have preeminence. Without Your loving leadership, I am incomplete. May nothing else replace the pleasure of Your company.

(Prayer taken from: Philippians 2:9; Ephesians 1:18–22; Revelation 2:4; Matthew 22:38; Colossians 1:17–18; Psalm 51:10–13; Hosea 2:14, 19; 1 Corinthians 13:1–3)

7

THE DECISION

Now as they were traveling along, [Jesus] entered a certain village; and a woman named Martha welcomed Him into her home. And she had a sister called Mary, who moreover was listening to the Lord's word, seated at His feet. But Martha was distracted with all her preparations; and she came up to Him, and said, "Lord, do You not care that my sister has left me to do all the serving alone? Then tell her to help me." But the Lord answered and said to her, "Martha, Martha, you are worried and bothered about so many things; but only a few things are necessary, really only one, for Mary has chosen the good part, which shall not be taken away from her."

Luke 10:38–42

This is one of my favorite passages of Scripture— and one of my least favorites. While it confirms the affections of my heart, it also convicts the decisions of my mind. I'm a Mary at heart, loving my quiet times and the moments when I find myself reveling in the Lord's presence. At other times, however, life forces me into Martha mode and I find myself trapped in the maze of a merciless schedule with seemingly no way out. Life is a constant balancing act, and too often the scales tip the wrong way. The most important things—God, family, and good health—are sometimes outweighed by the proverbial tyranny of the urgent. If we are not careful, the American Dream can become a nightmare. I'm sure those who live in other nations face similar challenges.

This passage concerning Mary and Martha is loaded with helpful insights to aid us in overcoming this tendency. To find these nuggets, we must dig below the surface and do a few word studies; but I assure you treasure buried there is well worth the effort. Let's begin with two Greek words used in the simple statement, "Mary . . . was listening to the Lord's word." "Listening" is *akouo*, and has a broad range of meanings, depending on its context. It can mean simply "to hear," but at times it carries the stronger meaning "to understand, hear with the ear of the mind; to hear effectively so as to perform what is spoken."

"Word" is *logos*, which is not the normal Greek term for spoken words (that would be *rhema*). *Logos*, which includes spoken words, has the added meaning of "connecting" or "linking" words in order to communicate thoughts and messages. *Logos*, therefore, embodies the logic that words are communicating—the content. It's easy to see the connection to our English word "logic," which is indeed derived from *logos*.

Mary was sitting quietly, listening intently to what Jesus was saying, and therefore was hearing more than mere words. She *understood* the *message* they were conveying. She was making the connection. Jesus' words were penetrating her heart and mind, bringing knowledge, creating paradigms, and shaping beliefs.

The Lego construction blocks kids play with are also a derivative of *logos*, and they present a great picture of what was occurring in Mary. Lego blocks connect in order to build structures—buildings, bridges, etc.—just as words do in order to build thoughts. The Lord's words were "connecting" in Mary, building a foundation for her life and creating a grid for her paradigms and beliefs.

Martha, on the other hand, was busy working. She was so busy, in fact, that the Lord said she was "distracted." The literal meaning of the Greek word used is much stronger than simply being distracted. In fact, the picture it communicates is brutal: "To drag around in circles."

Ouch! Busyness can be a real drag.

Okay, that was bad. But the point is important. Martha was more than just distracted. Her tendency toward busyness had gotten her life out of balance. While Mary was enjoying the *pleasure* of His company, Martha was experiencing the *pressure* of His company. It's one thing to experience the frustration of being unproductive; it's another thing to compound the lack of productivity with weariness by dragging around unnecessary weights. Ecclesiastes, the book of Scripture in which Solomon delineated his frustration with life, tells us, "God made us plain and simple, but we have made ourselves very complicated" (Ecclesiastes 7:29 GNT).

I've always felt the latter part of this verse is true of women. I've been told a time or two that the first part of it is true of us men. Actually, the verse is true with all of us. We allow life to get out of control and far too complex. We must de-complicate things. Paul said to the church at Corinth, "But I am afraid that, as the serpent deceived Eve by his craftiness, your minds will be led astray from the *simplicity* and purity of devotion to Christ" (2 Corinthians 11:3, italics mine).

While Mary was enjoying the simple pleasure of His company, Martha was allowing it to further complicate her life. Be like Mary—do some simplifying at His feet!

There is another word that adds tremendous insight to the Lord's gentle but revealing correction to Martha. Jesus told her she was distracted with all her "preparations." The word used here (*diakonia*) is also the Greek word for "ministry." In the Scriptures, there is no distinction made between serving or ministering to someone in a general sense, or doing so in what we've come to call "the ministry." As far as God is concerned, whether we're serving a family member, a friend, or a congregation, we're all ministers. Tell your friends to start calling you reverend!

The words used by the Holy Spirit in this passage were chosen carefully in order to convey a critical understanding: *No matter how important or noble our activities may be, including working* for *Him, they don't trump time* with *Him.* Nothing we could possibly do in life is more important than keeping Christ as our first priority. His words provide us with equilibrium—they keep our lives balanced. Like Legos, they form the beliefs, understanding, and wisdom we can use to build our lives. They provide structure and strength.

If our foundations are not laid with the strengths and wisdom found in His words, they will crack under pressure. The Lord used this analogy with Joshua as he was about to take over Moses' leadership role (see Joshua 1:1–9). What a daunting task! Jehovah told Joshua to carefully listen to His words and remember them, reminding Israel's new leader that they would bring him success and prosperity. The Lord then gave him an interesting command: "Do not tremble or be dismayed" (v. 9).

"Dismayed" is translated from the Hebrew word *chathath*, meaning "to break." Bible scholar Spiros Zodhiates says, "The meaning ranges from a literal breaking to abstract destruction, to demoralization, and finally to panic." He likens it to the concept we use nowadays of "cracking under stress."[1] God was telling Joshua to "chill out," to not let the stress get to him.

The Lord knew Joshua's assignment would be difficult. Possessing the land would be more demanding than camping in the wilderness. The latter involved the stress of day-to-day life; the former would add to this the struggles of war. The pressures on Joshua would have been extreme. How was he to keep from cracking under the stress? What would maintain freshness and joy? The solution would be listening to (*akouo*) and building with the words (*logos*) of God. For you and me it will be the same.

No matter how hectic your life has become, slow down for a few minutes each day and listen to Him. Get off the treadmill of life and spend some quality time enjoying the pleasure of His company. Let nothing stop you. With childlike simplicity, hang out with God.

Young Tommy had been an unexpected "bonus child" to his parents, and he continued to surprise and delight his family with his spontaneous expressions of love. Shortly after he had turned five, Tommy asked his mother, "How old were you when I was born?" Upon learning she had been thirty-six, he exclaimed, "What a shame!" A little puzzled, his mother asked him what he meant. Tommy's reply: "Just think of all those years we didn't know each other."[2]

Take a lesson from Tommy. Don't allow another day—let alone another year—to go by without getting to know Him intimately.

Prayer

How lovely is Your dwelling place, Father. It is there that My heart longs to be; learning of Your heart and Your ways, beholding Your majestic beauty.

I repent for letting the busyness of life keep me from the most important thing—time spent in devotion to Christ, in purity and simplicity. Jesus, I don't want to be a casual listener; I want to sit at Your feet and listen intently as You lovingly speak. Be it a loud trumpet call or a gentle whisper, I want to follow every leading of Your heart.

Father, I ask for wisdom and revelation, that I may truly come to know Your Son. Holy Spirit, help me to apply my heart to understand the messages the Father conveys, such that they'll penetrate and transform every part of me.

Let my life be founded upon the wisdom of Your Word that would lead me to walk in the fear of the Lord, lay all else aside in yieldedness, and abide with You, my King. Jesus, I choose to slow down today and invite You in for a time to connect heart to heart. Once again, let me enjoy the pleasure of Your company.

(Prayer taken from: Psalm 27:4; Luke 10:38–42; 1 Kings 19:12–13; Proverbs 2; 2 Corinthians 11:3; Hebrews 12:1; John 15:1–11)

8

THE DISTRACTIONS

In the previous chapter we began looking at the biblical account of Mary and Martha, two sisters who entertained Jesus in their home. While Martha was distracted as she prepared Him a meal, Mary was seated at the Lord's feet hearing and understanding His words. The passage is so pregnant with revelation it merits another look.

Now as they were traveling along, He entered a village; and a woman named Martha welcomed Him into her home. She had a sister called Mary, who was seated at the Lord's feet, listening to His word. But Martha was distracted with all her preparations; and she came up to Him and said, "Lord, do You not care that my sister has left me to do all the serving alone? Then tell her to help me." But the Lord answered and said to her, "Martha, Martha, you are worried and bothered about so many things; but only one thing is necessary, for Mary has chosen the good part, which shall not be taken away from her."

Luke 10:38–42

I've already acknowledged my tendency toward Martha-ism. I am important, after all! Someone once gave me a two-billed cap—one pointing left, the other right—imprinted with the words, "I'm their leader. Which way did they go?"

I still wear it proudly!

How sadly appropriate is this cap. There was a time when I needed only two of me to accomplish all of the "urgent" and "important" things I'm "called" to do. Now I need me in triplicate. And my Martha ministry is still growing—soon I'll need to be omnipresent!

Jesus disagreed with this outlook on ministry. In a loving yet stern way, He told Martha she was "worried and bothered about so many things" (v. 41). Not good, especially when we take a deeper look. "Worried" is *merimnao*, which has in its root meaning the concept of dividing or separating something. It is revealing that worry is defined by a "divided" mind. When we're worried about something, no matter how hard we try to focus on other things, a piece of our mind keeps being drawn back to our concern. Our mind, therefore, is described as being "divided into parts," a phrase used to define *merimnao*. Martha, it seems, had so much going on in her life that her mind was divided between many concerns; "so many things" was the phrase Jesus used. And like all of us at times, her balancing act wasn't working as well as she thought. She was "worried and bothered."

Martha was in all likelihood servant-motivated. She was probably one of those gifted people who can do several things at once, and was most likely a hard worker. In this instance, however, Mary had it right. Multitasking can be good, but not when Jesus is talking.

In an interview with *Today's Christian Woman,* writer and speaker Carol Kent says:

> One day when [my son] Jason was young, we were eating breakfast together. I had on an old pair of slacks and a fuzzy old sweater. He flashed his baby blues at me over his cereal bowl and said, "Mommy, you look so pretty today."
>
> I didn't even have makeup on! So I said, "Honey, why would you say I look pretty today? Normally I'm dressed up in a suit and high heels."
>
> Then he said, "When you look like that, I know you're going someplace; but when you look like this, I know you're all mine."[1]

The Lord appreciates hard work, and He knows that at times we're going to be very busy. But like Jason, He also wants times when we're all His. Take the cap off and sit for a while.

The word *bothered* is also painfully revealing. It is the Greek word *turbazo,* which is derived from the Latin word *turba*, meaning "a crowd." Webster says "disturb," "perturb," and "turbulent" are all derivatives of the same word.[2] When life gets too crowded we get disturbed. Perturbed comes next, followed by turbulence. Like an airplane flying through a storm, our emotions bounce up and down, making us short-tempered and irritable. Our health suffers, as do our relationships. Martha was not only irritated at Mary, she was even a little miffed at Jesus. "Do you not care that my sister has left me to do all the serving alone? Then tell her to help me," she grumbled. Barking out orders to God in accusatory language probably created just a little bit of turbulence in this room full of people!

Mary wasn't the problem, however, and Jesus certainly wasn't. Martha simply needed to take her cap off, slow down, and listen. Her crowded mind couldn't shut out all the noise. Many offices nowadays have ambient noise generators. They emit constant but quiet sound, low enough so as not to be disturbing, yet loud enough to drown out other noises. They're used in phone centers to drown out other voices, in counseling offices to provide privacy, and in various other businesses.

Martha's ambient noise generator was her service for Christ. Amazing, but true. Believe me, I understand. Her generator was the rattling of dishes, the banging of cupboards, and the clanging of utensils; my generator is the internal noise caused by travel, preaching and teaching, writing, leading a Bible school, correspondence, meetings, and more. All good, but not when they muffle the voice of the Master. Your ambient noise generator may be running a business, driving nails, keeping books, raising kids, social media, or even a hobby. It doesn't matter what it is, just turn it off once in a while.

Mary didn't have one of those contraptions. She was mesmerized by His words. Her attitude was, "If He wants something to eat, He'd better stop teaching. Because until He does, I'm not leaving this spot."

Why did Martha feel differently? Perhaps it was her personality, or could it be that Jesus had grown a little too familiar to her? Scholars agree that Jesus was very fond of Martha, Mary, and their brother, Lazarus, and stayed in their home when in the area. Had Martha heard Him enough that the excitement had worn off? Does this ever happen to us?

In *Christianity Today*, Philip Yancey writes:

> I remember my first visit to Old Faithful in Yellowstone National Park. Rings of Japanese and German tourists surrounded the geyser, their video cameras trained like weapons on the famous hole in the ground. A large, digital clock stood beside the spot, predicting 24 minutes until the next eruption.
>
> My wife and I passed the countdown in the dining room of Old Faithful Inn overlooking the geyser. When the digital clock reached one minute, we, along with every other diner, left our seats and rushed to the window to see the big, wet event.
>
> I noticed that immediately, as if on signal, a crew of busboys and waiters descended on the tables to

refill water glasses and clear away dirty dishes. When the geyser went off, we tourists oohed and aahed and clicked our cameras; a few spontaneously applauded. But, glancing back over my shoulder, I saw that not a single waiter or busboy—not even those who had finished their chores—looked out the huge window. Old Faithful, grown entirely too familiar, had lost its power to impress them.[3]

I'm afraid this describes many Christians' relationship with the one we call Faithful and True. We've known Him so long, become so accustomed to Him, well, you know . . .

Don't ever stop being impressed with Jesus!

It's interesting that those in this story who had lost their wonder over Old Faithful were "kitchen people"—just like Martha. Get out of the kitchen once in a while. Slow down. STOP!

Fight tenaciously for quality time at His feet and never lose your hunger for the pleasure of His company.

Prayer

Father, I thank You for never ceasing to communicate with me. But so often I let Your voice be drowned out by other noises and let other lovers steal from my time with You. I must get back to that which is most important. You are worthy of the highest affections of my heart.

Jesus, I thank You for responding to my repentant heart and drawing near to me. I desire to live wholly yielded with a pure heart that honors You in all things. May my heart be captivated by Your heart and mesmerized by Your words, over and over again.

The harsh yoke of busyness and heavy burden of over-activity, I take off now and lay down at Your cross. I can never let my health, disposition, or relationships suffer again at the mercy of life's disturbances—balance is what I need. Holy Spirit, help me to continually break away from the bustle and shut out all the noise.

Today I choose to cease from striving, so that with singleness of heart, I can rest at Your feet, Jesus, and be washed in Your words and Your love. May busyness never crowd out of my life precious opportunities to enjoy the pleasure of Your company.

(Prayer taken from: Luke 10:38–42; James 1:7–8, James 4:8; Psalm 86:11; Matthew 11:29–30; Psalm 46:10; Psalm 23:1–3)

9

THE CHOICE

I'm gonna blow your doors off!"

My frustration could no longer be contained on this particular morning's commute to teach at Christ For The Nations Institute in Dallas, Texas. I was running late that day, and as was often the case, my three-year-old daughter, Sarah, was with me so she could attend the preschool classes.

When we pulled out of our subdivision, we ended up behind an elderly man driving an old pickup truck at about twenty miles per hour. After following him for about five minutes on a country road that offered no opportunity to pass, we finally turned onto a four-lane highway. By this time I had totally lost my patience, and as I zoomed by his vehicle I mumbled, "Man, I'm gonna blow your doors off!"

Sarah was quiet for the next two or three miles, which I thought was rather unusual. Then, with great concern in her voice, she asked, "Daddy, why are you going to blow that man's doors off?" While watching *Sesame Street*, she had recently heard the story of *The Three Little Pigs* and the big bad wolf who blew their houses down. Now she was picturing me literally blowing the doors off this man's truck! She had obviously been thinking about this nonstop since hearing my exclamation, and was rather alarmed and puzzled.

Try explaining to a three-year-old why passing a car is described by some as "blowing their doors off." Then, of course, she needed to know that I really didn't dislike this elderly gentleman, just his driving.

A mile or so down the road, I passed another car and said, "Would you get out of my way?!"

"Daddy, who are you talking to?"

"The man in the car we just went around."

"Can he hear you?" she asked very sincerely.

"No, of course not," I replied.

"Then why are you talking to him?" was her next logical question.

I thought about explaining to her that it's a very sensible thing to do because it relieves stress and causes one's driving experience to be much more satisfying and peaceful, but I didn't think a three-year-old would understand such profound logic.

After this enlightening experience, I realized I would

need to be more careful about what I said. My children were listening to me.

Sometimes kids listen better than we adults. We've been looking at Martha's failure to listen to Christ as He taught in her home. Let's take one more look at this powerful passage. There are still a couple more pearls hidden in it that are just too good to pass up.

> Now as they were traveling along, He entered a village; and a woman named Martha welcomed Him into her home. She had a sister called Mary, who was seated at the Lord's feet, listening to His word. But Martha was distracted with all her preparations; and she came up to Him and said, "Lord, do You not care that my sister has left me to do all the serving alone? Then tell her to help me." But the Lord answered and said to her, "Martha, Martha, you are worried and bothered about so many things; but only one thing is necessary, for Mary has chosen the good part, which shall not be taken away from her."
>
> Luke 10:38–42

The Lord made an important statement to Martha, telling her that only a few things are really necessary in life. So far so good. Food, water, shelter from the elements, oxygen—the list of essentials really is short. Then He dropped the bombshell: "Really only one."

He had me, then He lost me.

I'm ready to admit that many of my "essentials" in life really are not. Most are for comfort, pleasure, or personal satisfaction. But the seemingly absurd claim that only one thing in life is really necessary is rather hard to swallow. But Jesus said it, and we have to deal with it.

Connecting the statement to Mary's decision to sit at the Lord's feet and listen to His words makes His meaning rather obvious. Here's my opinion of what Jesus meant: "Martha, if you will truly connect with Me, everything else in life will fall into place. Order will be established; relationships will make sense; I'll guide your steps into purpose and destiny; I'll teach you to prosper—*everything will work well if you'll simply listen to Me.*"

Jesus was either a very arrogant and self-deceived cult leader, which would mean we should look for truth somewhere else, or He was and is God, making Him the embodiment of truth. If He is the latter, and we believe He is, that makes His offer to Martha—and all of us, as well—one of the most amazing of all time. "All you really need to do in order to enjoy a successful and enjoyable life is listen to Me. The pleasure of my company will also be the source of your success, fulfillment, and well-being."

Astounding, incredible, wonderful, generous . . . and simple.

Yet life gets complicated. The pace quickens, the to-do list grows, and the Martha side of our nature kicks in. The voice of the Master is then drowned out by the pace of life. When this occurs, *and it will*, the solution is to return to the simple strategy of Mary: Sit and listen. Let's look again at what the apostle Paul said of the Corinthian church: "I am afraid that, as the serpent deceived Eve by his craftiness, your minds will be led astray from the *simplicity* and purity of devotion to Christ" (2 Corinthians 11:3, italics mine). Life truly can be complicated, but relationship with Jesus isn't.

The passage in Luke says that Mary "chose" the right activity. Most of us don't believe, or we don't take the time to consciously consider, that we always have the ability to choose the simple devotion demonstrated by Mary. But we do.

After informing Martha that only one thing was really necessary, Jesus then referred to Mary's choice as "good." That seems rather lame until the Greek word used is really understood. There are two Greek words that He could have used, *agathos* and *kalos*. *Kalos* means something is made well and looks good. It is even used for "beauty" or "handsome"; in our day we use the term "good-looking." *Kalos* can even include inner beauty or virtue. The word stops short, however, of suggesting practical usefulness. A good example of *kalos* would be a beautiful picture—it looks good but has no practical use.

When a word is needed, however, that adds the concept of usefulness or benefit, *agathos* is chosen. To fully convey this aspect, *agathos* is often translated "good works." Essentially, *kalos* is good looks, *agathos* is good works. Jesus said Mary chose *agathos*.

The irony of this is astounding. The person doing nothing was credited with doing the "good works," not the person doing all the good works! That ain't right, as we say in Texas. But it was, and it is. Christ was saying, "You look good, Martha, but your busyness won't produce the good works you're looking for. Mary chose that which will enable her to truly do good works, and her fruit will remain."

As one who gives his life to full-time ministry in the church, I am terrified by this passage. It shows me that I can be very busy in ministry without it producing genuine and lasting fruit. I can *look* good, without really *doing* good. We must always remember that it is Christ's life flowing through us that produces eternal fruit in others, not our abilities and self-chosen activities. I'm afraid all of us are seduced by this "good-looking" seductress once in a while.

Jesus warned a group of believers in Scripture that this was happening to them. "You have a name that you are alive, but you are dead," He said to the church of Sardis (Revelation 3:1). In order for these folks to maintain a reputation of being alive, they would have to still look fruitful. To the casual observer, their works must have been impressive. But the Lord looks not at our outward appearance, but at the heart (see 1 Samuel 16:7), and He judges our works based on their eternal significance, not on how they look to other people. His message to these believers was, "You're *kalos*, not *agathos*. Stop with all the busyness and choose the good part—Me."

Now that I've written myself into a state of deep conviction, I think I'll put pen and paper away and go listen for a while. Perhaps if I do, I can work less and accomplish more . . . and maybe even enjoy the pleasure of His company a little more often.

Prayer

Father, You are the source of all that is good—success, fulfillment, well-being. Thank You for giving me access through Your Son to an infinite fountain of blessing.

May I always remain in right relationship with You, Jesus, choosing the better thing—to sit at Your feet and abide in that place from which flourishes the good fruit of ministry.

Jesus, You are the vine—my lifeline—may I be properly aligned to Your heart. I need the order of heaven established in my life to walk out my destiny. Father, guide me by Your Holy Spirit to make choices each day that will steer me toward accomplishing the good works that long before time You prepared for me.

Good Shepherd, I choose to rest in Your abundance and drink from Your living waters. Let my heart never be led astray from a simple, pure, and steadfast devotion to Christ. May the pleasure of Your company always remain my favorite and first choice.

(Prayer taken from: Ephesians 1:3; Ephesians 2:10; Luke 10:38–42; Psalm 34:10; 2 Corinthians 11:3; John 15:1–11)

10

THE UNION

Unlike most of you impatient sinners, I love to wait. NOT! Ceci and my daughters have called me on the carpet for thirty years concerning my impatience. I, in turn, remind them of Scriptures on not being judgmental. Besides, I'm making progress—slowly. I mean, really, who enjoys waiting? There are several things I would fix immediately if I was put in charge of the world.

- Driving in the passing lane of a highway when not passing another vehicle would result in a $500 fine for a first-time offense, automatic loss of driver's license the second time. Retaking driver's education would be required in order to get it back. Actually, I might just make EVERYONE take (or retake or take for the first time) driver's education, even without this offense, then they all would know how to use BLINKERS.

- Cell phones would be programmed to self-destruct if operated while driving.

- Families or friends whose group stretches ALL THE WAY ACROSS THE TERMINAL CORRIDOR in airports, walking slowly, chitchatting and blocking those of us who have places to go and things to do, would lose all flying privileges. (Unless they took a walker's education class.)

- Folks who stand in check-out lines digging for pennies in the bottom of their purses would be charged an additional $100 for the purchase. Cashiers who visit with them while this is happening, making it worse, would be fired.

- People who cut lines would have to leave the country. Clerks, cashiers, and other workers who allow this instead of sending them to the end of the line would lose a week's pay; second offense—banished with the line-cutter.

- If one has to wait more than twenty minutes in a doctor's office before being treated, the visit is free. No exceptions. Second offense, they pay us for *our* time.

- Grown men and women who hide behind bushes, trees, buildings, and around curves with little radar guns, trying to catch those of us who legitimately break the speed limit because we're *too busy* to slow down, would be reprimanded and forced to start looking for *real* criminals or *real* jobs.

- I'd abolish the IRS. Anyone who has worked for the IRS would have to serve a taxpayer, without pay, for a year. (This has nothing to do with having to wait, I just hate being so over-taxed.)

It's easy to see that given the right opportunity, I could correct much of the injustice in the world and eliminate the stress caused by unnecessary waiting. These injustices aren't actually a big deal to me, by the way. For the most part, I'm a pretty well-adjusted, mild-mannered, cool, calm, and collected guy.

Okay, so I don't like waiting. Most of us don't. But there is one type of waiting I've learned to enjoy: waiting on God. Before you question my honesty, let me point out that I'm not talking about the type of waiting required when God chooses to delay doing something. Like you, I'm not into that. The waiting I enjoy is waiting in His presence.

The biblical concept of waiting on the Lord is understood by few people these days. Like many other biblical words, much is lost in the translation and because of the cultural differences that exist between nations and eras. Carefully defining three Old Testament words translated as "waiting" will give us clearer insight. The first one is *duwmiyah*, which means "silently waiting with a quiet trust." The thought conveyed is a strong, calm, quiet trust in the Lord. David said, "My soul waits in silence for God only; from Him is my salvation. He only is my rock and my salvation, My stronghold; I shall not be greatly shaken" (Psalm 62:1–2).

The second word, *chakah*, means "adhere to" or "long for." The psalmist said, "Our soul waits for the Lord; He is our help and our shield" (Psalm 33:20). The writer was clinging to the Lord, knowing that He would come through as a help in time of trouble. When David said, "My soul thirsts for God" (Psalm 42:2; 63:1), he was *chakah*—longing for God's company.

The third word, *qavah*, means to "wait for with eager expectation." Notice the combination of excitement and faith element in this definition. Our three dogs have learned the approximate time I come home from work, especially Gracie Mae, our coonhound. (All of Ceci's dogs have middle names.) When the time approaches, they wait with eager expectation. Those who *qavah* for the Lord are doing more than passively waiting; they're anticipating and expecting. Psalm 27:14 tells us, "Wait for the Lord; Be strong and let your heart take courage; Yes, wait for the Lord."

Another powerful meaning of *qavah* exists, however: "to bind together by twisting," as in a braid or a rope. As we spend time with the Lord, a joining of hearts occurs, creating oneness of desires, thinking, and actions. This is what transforms the mission of one into a co-mission involving two or more. Causes are shared, becoming movements, and passions are shared, creating energy and action.

Another result of braiding is increased strength. Isaiah said, "Yet those who wait (*qavah*) for the Lord will gain new strength; They will mount up with wings like eagles, They will run and not get tired, They will walk and not become weary" (Isaiah 40:31).

The renewing of strength this verse promises is the result of being braided together with God. When the strands of a rope are braided into one, the strength of each strand is transferred to the other. When we wait on God, His strength is transferred to us and vice versa. Guess who gets the better deal? It sort of reminds me of the mouse and elephant who were best friends. They hung out together all the time, the mouse riding on the elephant's back. One day they crossed a wooden bridge, causing it to bow, creak, and sway under their combined weight. After they were across, the mouse, impressed over their ability to make such an impact, said to the elephant, "We sure shook up that bridge, didn't we?"

Guess who the mouse is?

Let's summarize these three meanings of biblical waiting, combining them into one complete definition of waiting on the Lord: *Quietly waiting with a strong, calm trust; longing for His presence and eagerly expecting Him, for you know He'll come; and knowing that as He does, you and He will experience an increased oneness, a braiding together, as your hearts and lives become more entwined.*

That's what I'm talking about! If that doesn't float your boat, you need a new boat.

David, the psalmist who wrote so much about waiting on God, practiced it as a young shepherd and was then empowered to kill a lion, a bear, and a giant. Where did he get such amazing strength and prowess? By riding the elephant's back. He curled up in God's lap for a while, then wrote beautiful poems like the Twenty-third Psalm. At times he and the Lord became so one through waiting that God's foreknowledge seeped into David's mind, allowing him to prophesy the future. One of many examples is Psalm 22, which has three of the seven sayings of Christ while on the cross.

God gives revelation to, strengthens, comforts, guides, and blesses those who wait on Him. Every need found in our humanness can be met by connecting to His divineness. Wait on Him.

Practically speaking, what describes this type of activity? Do we sit quietly, trying to enter a trancelike state wherein we can more easily enter the spirit realm? No, we're not Buddhists or transcendentalists. The meditation process taught in Scripture—which certainly is a form of waiting on God—is not an altered state of consciousness. It is simply musing on, thinking about, or reflecting on God or a passage of Scripture.

Waiting can be done while sitting, kneeling, walking, lying down, driving—it isn't the position of the body that matters but the posture of the heart. It may be done through prayer, worship, or contemplative thinking. There is nothing complicated about it. A quality "quiet time" is a means of waiting on the Lord. Make it enjoyable—sit with a cup of coffee and visit with Him. I've sat in front of a fire for hours enjoying the pleasure of His company. For me, it doesn't get any better than that.

I'm not implying, however, that times with the Lord have to last for hours to be effective. Quality is more important than quantity. I've received great revelation and insight from the Holy Spirit in as little as fifteen to twenty minutes of visiting with Him. It is also important to do it with regularity. All of us should have regular quiet times of waiting on the Lord that are shorter, whether they be thirty minutes or an hour, and all of us should occasionally spend longer times with Him.

Learn to wait. In this hectic world of microwaves, bullet trains, and air travel, there are some things that still take time. Slow down. If only for a few minutes a day—slow down and find Him. I promise you that if you will, you'll live longer . . . and you'll live better.

Prayer

Father, You are worth waiting for; deserving of my lingering and longing with eager expectation for the gift of Your sweet presence.

Help me to become familiar with the art of silently waiting on You in a strong, calm, quiet trust. Bind my heart tenaciously to Yours, Father, as I abide in the place where You are. I want to be one with You in thought and desire, reflecting the glory of Your Son.

Jesus, how precious is Your steadfast love. As I wait, You fill me with profound joy and strengthen me deep within. When I take refuge in You I am comforted and find the safest place of rest.

Right now I choose to slow down and posture my heart to wait. Echoing the prayer of the psalmist, this one thing will I seek: to dwell in Your house all the days of my life, meditating, gazing, simply beholding every facet of Your beauty . . . enjoying the pleasure of Your company.

(Prayer taken from: Psalm 62:1–2; Psalm 27:14; Isaiah 40:31; Psalm 16:11; Psalm 21:6; Psalm 27:4)

11

THE SPOILER

One of the greatest offers in the history of the world was made centuries ago to a man named Obed-edom. At the instruction of David, king of Israel, he was asked if his living room could be the Holy of Holies for a while.

> And David was unwilling to move the ark of the Lord into the city of David with him; but David took it aside to the house of Obed-edom the Gittite. Thus the ark of the Lord remained in the house of Obed-edom the Gittite three months, and the Lord blessed Obed-edom and all his household.
>
> 2 Samuel 6:10–11

Can you imagine being asked, "Would you mind if we placed the ark of the covenant in your home for a few months?" If you were a lover of God, this honor would have been unimaginable. Remember, in Obed-edom's day, it was over the ark that the very glory of God hovered.

How would you respond? "Uh, I don't know, King. I'll have to think about whether or not I want the shekinah glory of God hovering in my living room for the next three months." I don't think I'd have had to pray about it. Obviously, Obed-edom didn't.

Can you imagine locating your wife and blurting out, "You'll never guess what is in our living room!" And what about the conversation with your kids: "Now, guys, you can look but DON'T TOUCH!" And don't you just imagine that his house became the first choice for the neighborhood home group!

One can only guess what it was like at Obed-edom's home for the three months the ark was there. Did they sit for hours and stare at it? Did it ever get dark in the house? (Think about it.) Was the whole house permeated by the presence of God? Was there a constant haze? Did people fall down when they walked by it? We don't know the answers to these questions, but we do know "the Lord blessed Obed-edom and all his household" (v. 11) during this unprecedented season. We also know that when David finally moved the ark of the covenant to Jerusalem, Obed-edom packed up and moved his entire household with it, becoming a gatekeeper in the tent that housed it (1 Chronicles 26:1–4). One can almost hear his conversation with David: "If you think, Your Highness, that after having the presence and glory of God in my living room for the last three months I'm going to live without it, you're badly mistaken. You're taking me with you!"

The Lord must have been excited to finally have some people in Israel who appreciated and wanted His presence. Incredibly, the ark hadn't been the focal point of worship in Israel for decades. The reason for this went all the way back to the days of a high priest named Eli, whose leadership allowed such sin into Israel that God allowed the ark to be stolen by the Philistines. It was then that the well-known word *ichabod*, meaning "no glory," came about:

> Now [Eli's] daughter-in-law, Phinehas's wife, was pregnant and about to give birth; and when she heard the news that the ark of God was taken and that her father-in-law and her husband had died, she kneeled down and gave birth, for her pains came upon her. And about the time of her death the women who stood by her said to her, "Do not be afraid, for you have given birth to a son." But she did not answer or pay attention. And she called the boy Ichabod, saying, "The glory has departed from Israel," because the ark of God was taken and because of her father-in-law and her husband. She said, "The glory has departed from Israel, for the ark of God was taken."
>
> 1 Samuel 4:19–22

The Philistines attempted to place the ark in the temple of their god Dagon, but the Lord visited such judgment on them that they happily sent it back to Israel (1 Samuel 5–6). It ended up in Kiriath-jearim, where it remained for twenty years (1 Samuel 7:2), until David became king.

It was David, a lover of God, who decided to go after the ark and bring it to Jerusalem. "Then David consulted with . . . every leader. And David said to all the assembly of Israel . . . 'Let us bring back the ark of our God to us, for we did not seek it in the days of Saul'" (1 Chronicles 13:1–3). What a sad epitaph for a leader: "The presence of God was not sought after during his reign." And what sad days those must have been for the Lord.

I'm certain He was pleased when David, a man after His heart, wanted Him and His presence to be the focal point of the nation once again. Yet the process turned out to be difficult. Due to the inappropriate way the ark was transported, a man felt compelled to touch it in an attempt to steady it. He was killed by the Lord, which resulted in a three-month delay. This is when it made its way to Obed-edom's house.

Finally, David discovered the correct way to transport the ark and it was relocated to Jerusalem. Obed-edom, however, was not about to buy into the separation. "Pack up, guys," he told the family. "We're moving."

I've done the Obed-edom thing—sort of. Obviously, it wasn't exactly the same but was about as close as you could get to it nowadays. Four years ago we had a special series of meetings in the church I pastored in

Colorado Springs. On Sunday morning, a prophetic guest dropped the bombshell. "Put everything else on hold and for ninety days do nothing but twenty-four/seven worship. Just as Obed-edom hosted the ark of His presence for three months, God is asking you to do the same," he declared.

I'm sure I blanched. After all, he said it publicly!

From the fact that I asked this man to speak, it's obvious I believe in prophecy, holding the view that God still speaks through people today. So it didn't surprise me that he was prophesying; I was expecting that. It was the radical nature of the assignment—shut down everything else and sustain 24/7 worship—and the fact that I didn't have the freedom to decide secretly whether or not I believed it was truly from the Holy Spirit that intimidated me. After all, the entire congregation heard it![1]

My mind started racing: Was this really a word from the Holy Spirit? Should we try it? Could we pull it off? What about our other programs? How would this affect the church? These and other questions flooded my mind. But . . .

We did it! We did the Obed-edom thing.

The next three months became the best of my life. Like Obed-edom, I'm spoiled. The logistics were challenging, of course, but the worship never stopped. And the presence of God in our sanctuary for the next ninety days, well, it was thick and weighty. I cancelled most of my speaking engagements during the three months and spent several hours every day just hanging out with God.

Not only did it change my life, it changed the lives of hundreds others. People took their vacation days and spent them with God. Occasionally, families brought sleeping bags and spent the night, camping out in His presence. Many came on their lunch breaks. A few people spent time with Him there *every* day; one lady actually spent every night there. An air force colonel came every night after work. At the end, we were all ruined. Normal, for us, had become radical. Thirty minutes and a few choruses on a Sunday morning would never again satisfy. The Obed-edom thing causes BIG problems. It's easy now to see why Obed-edom didn't even try to fight it. "I'm addicted," he said with his actions. "Where the ark goes, I go."

David seemed to understand. "No sense in arguing with him; he's been infected. He'll never outgrow or outlive it. Make him a doorkeeper at the tent." He, too, had this "disease." I finally understood how he could say, "A day in Your courts is better than a thousand outside" (Psalm 84:10). David also said, "One thing I have asked from the Lord, that I shall seek: That I may dwell in the house of the Lord all the days of my life, to behold the beauty of the Lord and to meditate in His temple" (Psalm 27:4).

I can relate.

The Song of Solomon, also known as the Song of Songs, is an allegory that depicts the relationship between Christ and His bride, the church. In it, there is a fascinating scene in which the groom (Christ) hides

Himself from His bride (the church). The interpretation for us is that Christ is precious, not a cheap thrill, and wants us to value Him enough to seek Him. In the Song, the bride passes the test, frantically searching for the groom, demonstrating her passion and commitment. She searches all through the night declaring, "I must seek him whom my soul loves" (3:2). Upon finding Him she says, "I held on to him and would not let go" (3:4).

You, too, can do the Obed-edom thing. No, not 24/7, but nonetheless, the Lord wants to come to your house. His presence is no longer limited to an ark in a Holy of Holies. Pursue Him. If you do, like the bride in the Song of Solomon, He'll let you find Him. Oh, how He wants to be found. Until you experience this pleasure, you'll never really understand it. Once you have, you'll never again be without it.

Prayer

Father, I've tasted and seen of Your goodness, and I hunger and thirst for much more. I want to host You and Your presence—may My heart be a fitting home for You, Lord.

Jesus, let me encounter Your heart to such an extent that I would be ruined for anything less—a bondservant cleaving unto You with deep conviction, declaring, "You're all I want and need!" Come, Lord Jesus, show me Your glory, reveal Yourself unto me. Thank You for letting Yourself be found by those who seek You wholeheartedly.

I must seek Him whom my soul loves with every mounting day. And when I find You, I will not let go. For one day with You, Jesus, is so much better than a thousand spent anywhere else.

May dwelling in the Father's house and beholding the beauty of Jesus be my highest aspiration, my greatest fascination, and the deepest longing of my heart. Let all things pale in comparison to time spent in the pleasure of Your company.

(Prayer taken from: Psalm 34:10; Matthew 5:6; Exodus 33:18–19; 2 Chronicles 15:15; Deuteronomy 4:29; Song of Solomon 3:2, 4; Psalm 84:10; Psalm 27:4)

12

THE PLACE

I love the mountains. Doesn't matter if it's to hunt, fish, walk, or sit—I just love hanging out in hills and mountains. I've spent hundreds of hours climbing hills, hiking majestic peaks, and sitting in lush valleys reflecting, relaxing, and rejuvenating my inner person. If you've never sat at the edge of a 13,000- or 14,000-foot mountain peak on a clear, sunny day looking over forests, rivers, lakes, and valleys—well, let's just say your bucket list is incomplete.

I remember the day seven years ago while hunting for elk in Colorado. Actually, I wasn't elk hunting; I was "view hunting." I had walked an hour or so from the truck when I rounded a turn, crested a hill, and . . . there it was. Several hundred yards below me was a gorgeous stream. Across the stream was a beautiful green hillside, covered with flowers, leading up into a golden aspen forest. Indescribable beauty! Almost surreal. *Well, this is it,* I thought. *My hunt is over. I couldn't find a better place to sit and talk to God.*

"How's it going today, Papa?" I asked. "It sure is great to be together here in this amazing setting."

I sat there for a while thinking and conversing with Dad, just enjoying the pleasure of His company. After a half hour or so, I heard the unmistakable screech of a golden eagle. Sure enough, there it was, soaring right in front of me—gliding, dipping, flying over the river then back above the trees—just showing off.

"How do you like that, son?" Papa God asked after a while.

"Awesome, Dad. Incredible performance," I said, congratulating Him.

If any of you have biblical proof that God would not have caused this eagle airshow and then spoken to me in this way, please don't share it with me. Leave me in my blissful ignorance. What a day!

As much as I love mountains, I don't like being alone on one in the dark. They get a little scary at that time of day. The absence of light awakens fright, and thrills give way to chills. There are wolves, grizzlies, black bears, and mountain lions behind every bush, just waiting to eat me. And you can get lost, really lost, on a mountain in the dark. So I make sure I'm back to the truck by nightfall.

Having experienced the intimidation of a mountain alone at night causes me to be even more impressed with

Joshua and his *thirty-four days alone on Mount Sinai.* Many people know Moses spent forty days and nights with God on this mountain, receiving the Ten Commandments and other laws, precepts, and religious rites God intended Israel to live by. Almost no one, however, knows about Joshua. But he was there, also.

God instructed Moses to join Him on this fiery mountain and he obeyed, taking Joshua, his servant, with him.

> Now the Lord said to Moses, "Come up to Me on the mountain and remain there, and I will give you the stone tablets with the law and the commandment which I have written for their instruction. So Moses arose with Joshua his servant, and Moses went up to the mountain of God. But to the elders he said, 'Wait here for us until we return to you. And behold, Aaron and Hur are with you; whoever has a legal matter, let him approach them.'"
>
> Exodus 24:12–14

Moses obeyed, taking Joshua, and up they went. Then things get really puzzling. God actually made the two of them wait *six full days* before He said anything. "And on the seventh day He called to Moses from the midst of the cloud" (v. 16). Can you imagine? What would you do for six days sitting just outside of a cloud caused by the glory of God, with thunder crashing and lightning flashing inside of it? The mountain actually shook at times. I wonder if Joshua ever asked, "Hey, Moses, are you *sure* we're supposed to be here?" We're not told what they did for six days, or why God made them wait.

Perhaps He was teaching them patience. Finally, however, He spoke from within the glory cloud and invited Moses in.

The part of this story that grabs me the most, however, is that on the seventh day when Moses disappeared into the glory cloud, *Joshua was left alone for thirty-four more days!* He wasn't invited to the party. One can only imagine what it was like to be there alone for more than a month. Was he horrified when Moses walked into the cloud? It was more than just a cloud, after all; it was a *fiery* cloud: "To the eyes of the sons of Israel [from the base of the mountain] the appearance of the glory of the Lord was like a consuming fire on the mountain top" (v. 17). One has to wonder:

- Did Joshua question for thirty-four days if Moses survived?
- Could he hear God and Moses talking?
- Did he flinch every time the mountain shook?
- Could he hear the finger of God chipping the Ten Commandments into the tablets?
- Did he ever get hungry? If so, what did he eat?
- Was he tempted to leave? (We know he didn't. Exodus 32:17 tells us they came down together.)
- Did Joshua sit for hours just staring at the glory?
- Did he have angelic visitations?
- Perhaps, while Dad was with Moses, was Jesus or the Holy Spirit visiting Joshua?
- What did he think when Moses finally emerged with his face glowing from glory exposure?

For reasons we don't know, God chose not to answer any of our questions. He knows that sometimes leaving us with unanswered questions creates healthy musings; at other times the silence is to honor the privacy of His personal dealings with individuals. What happened with Joshua will remain his and God's secret. What we do know is that while Moses was in the cloud for thirty-four days, Joshua was on the outside and, humanly speaking, alone.

Although God didn't tell us what transpired, He did give us a hint of the effect this excursion had on Joshua. In Exodus 32, Joshua and Moses came off the mountain. In chapter 33, Moses erected a tent, sometimes called the tabernacle of Moses, in which the ark of the covenant was to reside. It was also called the tent of meeting, for "everyone who sought the Lord would go out to the tent of meeting" (Exodus 33:7).

When Moses would go into the tent, the people were so captivated and spellbound, they would stand and watch, for "the pillar of the cloud would descend and stand at the entrance of the tent" (v. 9). This was so spellbinding and awe-inspiring that the people would "arise and worship, each at the entrance of his tent" (v. 10).

Everyone but Joshua, that is.

It would appear that on these occasions, Joshua was allowed to go into the tent with Moses. But something interesting took place when it was time for Moses to leave. "Thus the Lord used to speak to Moses face to face, just as a man speaks to his friend. When Moses returned to the camp, his servant Joshua, the son of Nun, a young man, *would not depart from the tent*" (v. 11, italics mine).

Joshua had been infected by an insatiable attraction to the God of glory. He was forever ruined on the mountain. He became like Obed-edom, who hosted the ark in his home for three months; he became so addicted to the presence of God surrounding it that when it was relocated to Jerusalem, he moved his entire family there. Joshua had become hopelessly enamored with the pleasure of His company. One can almost hear him asking his mentor and boss, Moses, as he was leaving, "Would it be all right if I stayed for a little while and hung out in the presence?"

I can imagine the other "addict" answering with a knowing smile, "Sure, son, take your time." It takes one to know one.

This type of addiction to God's presence doesn't occur overnight. When we begin our journey with Him, it takes a while to overcome the restlessness of our flesh and emotions as we wait on Him. The "unusualness" of relating to an invisible person must also be dealt with. It's almost as though our hearts have to learn to connect with His untouchable presence and our minds to be quiet enough to hear. In a world filled with sounds, people, and a myriad of activities, we must enter the school of the Holy Spirit, where we are instructed in the art of waiting. Joshua received a crash course on the mountain.

One of the things that will help in this process is to find or create a place where you meet with God regularly. This might be a room in your house, a rocker in the corner, a woods you walk in, a beach you stroll on, or a tree you sit under. Wherever it may be, there is something about setting apart a special place where you and God enjoy regular, undisturbed, face-to-face communion.

Moses had one, as did Joshua. David erected a tent for the same purpose. Even Christ had one, as the following Scriptures make clear.

> It happened that while Jesus was praying in *a certain place* . . .
>
> Luke 11:1, italics mine

> And He came out and proceeded *as was His custom* to the Mount of Olives . . . and when He arrived at *the place* . . .
>
> Luke 22:39–40, italics mine

This location was the garden of Gethsemane on the Mount of Olives, a place where Christ loved to pray. Many scholars believe that the fact that this was Christ's regular place of prayer while in Jerusalem was how Judas knew where to find Him when betraying Him (see Luke 22:47). Isn't it revealing that when Jesus was about to face His greatest trial and the brutality of the cross, He retreated to His "place" of communion and prayer?

Find or create a place where you meet with God. Then, if you haven't already, experiment with various translations of Scripture until you find the one you enjoy the most. Buy a journal and, as you spend time with Him, write down your thoughts. He will speak to you in your heart and through your mind. Some people also like to create a personal list of their favorite worship songs to listen to as they spend time with God.

Create the routine that works best for you and get started. If you choose to set aside these times visiting with Him and train your heart and mind to listen, you'll begin to hear His voice. Then you'll experience the reason you were created—to enjoy a true relationship with your heavenly Father. As happened with Joshua, an addiction will soon develop and your encounters with Him will become the highlight of every day. In fact, you'll find them so fulfilling that, like him, you won't want to leave the tent.

Prayer

Father, I love the house where You live, the place where Your glory dwells. I want to learn to abide in this place and enjoy a close-knit relationship with You.

Instruct me in how to practice the presence of God—cultivating the art of waiting on and communing with You, without interruption and often. Bring me into the school of the Holy Spirit where I'll learn to overcome the restlessness of my flesh—intentionally pulling away to join myself to You with my mind quieted to listen and my heart fully aware of and engaged with Your presence.

Just as You, Jesus, frequented a certain place to commune with the Father and pray, let me not rest until I find a special place to visit with You face-to-face—my sacred tent of meeting as in Joshua or David's day. And as I spend time in our special place, let me be infected with an insatiable attraction to Your glory that forever ruins me. Let me become one hopelessly enamored with the pleasure of Your company.

(Prayer taken from: Psalm 26:8; Psalm 27:4, 8; Acts 7:45–46; Exodus 33:7; Luke 11:1; Luke 22:39–40; Psalm 42:1–2)

13

THE WALK

I love to walk. I also like to explore. When I hunt, which I also like to do, I mostly walk around and check out the sights. This diminishes my effectiveness, since the animals are so adept at seeing movement and hearing noises, but I don't mind. For me, the thrill is in the hunt itself—the search, the exploration—not in the harvesting of the animal. When I see a hill, something in my psyche simply has to know what's on the other side. When the trail ahead turns, I have to know what is around the bend. My hunting friends usually query me when I arrive back at the truck, "How far did you go?" They know I can't sit still.

The farthest I've walked in one day while hunting, at least that I know of, is just over twenty miles. I know this because one of the fellas with me measured it using his GPS. On this particular day, such a long walk wasn't planned. We were scouting the area, looking for the best ways in and out of different locations.

We were confident there was a road at the base of the hill we were standing on, but the woods were too thick to see the bottom. We debated for a few minutes whether to make the descent—if we were wrong, the climb all the way back up the steep mountain would be grueling. I like walking, not climbing. But since approaching the area from the bottom would be by far the easiest, and confident of the road's existence, we decided to take the risk.

We were wrong. Way wrong.

I can't begin to tell you just how wrong we were. There was no road. It was gorgeous, with lush meadows bordering aspen trees and a beautiful mountain stream, but there was no road. Thinking perhaps we would find this nonexistent road if we followed the stream, we walked a couple of miles. Eventually, we happened upon another hunter on the edge of the stream. Relieved, we conversed for a while, then asked him where the road was.

"What road?" he responded.

"The road out of here."

"There is no road out of here," he answered.

"There has to be," we insisted, our concern mounting.

"My dad and I have been hunting here for twenty-five years," he said, "and I guarantee you there is no road into here."

"How did you get here?" we wondered, still unwilling to believe him.

"Horseback. We pack in and camp for the week."

We told him where we had parked at the top of Black Mountain, and asked him how to get to it. With a slight grin and a confident demeanor, he pointed to a trail that we could see meandered several miles up the mountain. "Up that trail, boys," he said. "That's the only way out of here. That's why they call it Hell Hole."

Shocked and not a little panicky, we said, "We have to be out by dark!" It was around noon at that time.

He gave us a warning smile and a piece of advice: "Then you'd better get going."

We made it just before dark with sore feet, tired legs, and bragging rights: We'd been to "hell" and back. Actually, it wasn't that bad for a walker. And it was so gorgeous I've always wanted to go back. Hey, if you wanna make the memory, you gotta take the walk! (Excuse my Texan slang, but sometimes it just works better.) If a person planned ahead, packed a lunch and plenty of water, it wouldn't be all that bad. And the peaceful meadow nestled up against the beautiful mountain stream—well, it was without doubt one of the prettiest places I've ever seen. The higher we climbed on our way out, the more beautiful the view of the stream and meadows became. Hell Hole had become a heavenly view, one I'll never forget. Perspective is everything.

Enoch was a walker. Perhaps you've heard of him. He was the guy who brought Yahweh such pleasure He decided to go ahead and translate him to heaven: "And Enoch walked with God; and he was not, for God took him," (Genesis 5:24). One day he was there, the next day he wasn't. I wonder if anyone saw him vanish, or get in the fiery chariot if the Lord took him in the manner he took Elijah. How would you like to try explaining it to your friends? I don't think so.

The concept of Enoch walking with God is a fascinating one. The word used can mean several things. It describes the flowing of a river, the descending of a flood, the blowing of the wind, the tossing of the sea, and, of course, walking. The basic idea is movement. It is used metaphorically to speak of the pathways of one's life. For example, a son can "walk in" or "follow after" the ways of a father.

Enoch followed after God and His ways, walking with Him on the pathway of his life. The meaning is quite simple: He lived life with God. Not satisfied with the mundane existence of life without God, Enoch decided to prioritize and enjoy the pleasure of His company. Somehow he knew walking with God was a decision *he* had to make—not God. The Scriptures don't say "God walked with Enoch," although that obviously occurred as they spent time together. No, the wording is important and the point is clear: "Enoch walked with God."

The Scriptures do tell us how the Lord felt about this relationship, however. The New Testament says of Enoch: "He obtained the witness that before his being taken up he was pleasing to God" (Hebrews 11:5).

"Pleasing" is from the Greek word *euarestos*. "Well-pleasing" would be a more accurate translation; the prefix *eu* means "well" or "good," and *arestos* means "to please." Seeing other people gloat over their grandkids has always been pleasing (*arestos*) to me. Now, having my own grandson is well-pleasing (*euarestos*). Enoch was more than pleasing to God, he was well-pleasing.

This hyphenated word isn't used much nowadays. A more contemporary way of describing Enoch's relationship to God would simply be that he brought Him great pleasure. Fascinating, isn't it? What is for us "the pleasure of *His* company," can become for God "the pleasure of *our* company." For most, this is an unheard-of concept. It's one thing to believe God can use us. And believing that our obedience to His laws pleases Him? No problem. But I can't help but wonder how many people realize their presence can bring pleasure to the Lord.

Don't be deceived into thinking that only a few spiritual elites like Enoch could possibly have such a relationship with the Lord. Paul said to the Corinthians, "We also have as our ambition . . . to be [well-]pleasing (*euarestos*) to Him" (2 Corinthians 5:9). A literal rendering of the latter part of Hebrews 12:28 would read, "Let us have gratitude, by which we can offer to God well-pleasing (*euarestos*) worship with reverence and awe." It absolutely is possible to become a pleasure to Father God. When this is understood, it transforms our lives. We step into a high calling, beginning a love affair with the One who made us in His own image and likeness. God created us as His family, with the capability of truly knowing and understanding Him. When this is understood, life becomes an exciting and glorious journey upward, not a Hell Hole to descend into. We have a destiny to fulfill, not an existence to waste.

Whatever else you do today, whether that be making money, enjoying someone else's company, or simply having a little fun, be sure to spend some quality time with Him. You were made for His pleasure. Make the walk!

Prayer

Father, how astounding the thought that this walking in rhythm with the beat of Your heart gives rise to such great pleasures within You, my God.

I want to be found always pleasing, bringing joy and delight to You, Lord. Help me to prioritize, reroute, and walk tirelessly, following the ways of Your heart. May the cry from within me be as Moses': "I'll only move forth if You do."

Father, work in me through Your Son, Jesus, that which is well-pleasing in Your sight. Instruct me in the way I should go—bearing fruit from good works, growing in the knowledge of God, being diligent to show myself approved. I choose to be led along on the wilderness pathway that brings honor and glory to You.

May pleasing You, Father, be my life's greatest ambition, such that when my life on this side of eternity ends, it would be said of me that I walked faithfully with God, choosing to offer Him the pleasure of my company.

(Prayer taken from: Genesis 5:24; 2 Corinthians 5:9; Hebrews 12:28; Hebrews 11:5; Romans 14:17–18; Exodus 33:15; Colossians 1:10; Psalm 32:8; Hebrews 13:20–21)

14

THE OFFERING

Like most of you, I've had my share of awkward moments.

- Congratulating the pregnant lady who wasn't pregnant (when I was young and stupid).
- Forgetting names (I'm notorious for that).
- Greeting as a married couple two people who were indeed married—but not to each other.
- Introducing a person to a friend by the wrong name.
- Showing up at a church to speak when they were not expecting me (scheduling mess-up by a third party).
- And, of course, every guy's worst fear—my fly unzipped in public.

I've had much worse, but I'll preserve a little dignity. Jesus, too, had some awkward moments—at least the situations would have created awkwardness for most of us. In His inimitable style, He didn't seem to be bothered by them. One of the worst had to be the uninvited attention He received from a prostitute.

Jesus had been invited to dinner at the house of a Pharisee (Luke 7:36–50). As the religious elites of their day, the Pharisees were proud, legalistic, and condescending to the common man. Always willing to point out their hypocrisy, Christ had more than one run-in with members of their sect. It was this group, in fact, that led the movement to crucify Him. This Pharisee was obviously not a believer in Christ's messiahship, but merely a curious skeptic trying to disprove the Lord's credentials. With their critical spirit and skeptical mindset, the Pharisees were notorious for this.

As they were eating, a woman described simply as a "sinner" showed up unannounced and uninvited. The margin note in my Bible calls her "an immoral woman," and most scholars believe she was actually a prostitute. You can imagine the shock and indignation of this self-righteous Pharisee when a "hooker" walked into his home—the text makes it clear he knew her lifestyle. But his indignation went to another level when she proceeded with her intentions.

> And behold, there was a woman in the city who was a
> sinner; and when she learned that He was reclining at

the table in the Pharisee's house, she brought an alabaster vial of perfume, and standing behind Him at His
feet, weeping, she began to wet His feet with her tears,
and kept wiping them with the hair of her head, and
kissing His feet and anointing them with the perfume.

Luke 7:37–38

Awkward!

I'm not sure how embarrassed I would be if a known
prostitute showed up at dinner and, *in front of a roomful
of people*, began bathing and kissing my feet, then drying
them with her hair. I'm sure I would stop her very quickly
and assure everyone that I had never met this person. Concern for my reputation would outweigh my compassion.

Jesus, however, didn't seem to mind. He was not embarrassed by this extravagant display of affection from a
desperate woman of the street. It seems, in fact, that He
welcomed and was moved by her actions, seeing them
as repentance and a cry for help—not an inappropriate
proposition. And He was always moved by a sincere, hungry heart. After a short dialogue with the pious Pharisee,
Jesus pronounced him rude and the prostitute forgiven;
her pure, him defiled. That would infuriate the average
pharisaical heart, wouldn't it? The Lord didn't care. The
worship of a penitent prostitute was far more fulfilling
to Him than a meal with a patronizing Pharisee.

The perfume used by this woman was myrrh, a
very aromatic and costly oil used for important occasions. Jesus, for example, was given myrrh by the magi,

117

sometimes called wise men, at His birth. The aroma of myrrh was strong enough that Christ would have carried the fragrance of the woman's act of worship with Him as He went on His way. I'm sure it brought the Savior great pleasure. Every time He caught the scent He smelled a changed life, a restored purpose, and a new member of His heavenly family.

Perhaps He thought of Psalm 45, which foretells His marriage to the church, His bride. He certainly would have been familiar with them. Verse 8 of this psalm says that at His wedding, His garments will carry the fragrance of myrrh. The Song of Solomon, which most Christian scholars agree is an allegory picturing Christ and His bride, also speaks much of the fragrance of myrrh in the bedchamber (see Song of Solomon 5:1, 5, 13).

Could it be that this prostitute, who was probably used to myrrh in her "trade," was acquainted with these popular portions of Scripture? Were her penitent tears, mixed with the fragrant myrrh, the passionate cry of a shame-filled sinner wondering if she could ever be accepted as part of His eternal bride? I like to think so.

And the response of the Bridegroom? "I still want you. Your defilement is gone, your sins forgiven, and your shame removed. You're beautiful to me." The *former* harlot left the house betrothed to the Savior, while the satisfied Pharisee left the occasion still playing the harlot with the religious system he was in bed with.

Jesus responds to love, not religion; to hunger, not curiosity. He is looking for those who want the *pleasure* of His company, not the *entertainment* of His company. His heart was moved, not by a sumptuous meal with a curious stranger but by the hungry heart of a common sinner. The curious may sow a meal, but the desperate will sow their tears . . . and, of course, perfume.

Toward the end of Christ's ministry, another worshiper poured costly perfume on the head and feet of Jesus (John 12:1–8). It was very expensive, worth a year's wages based on the average income of the day. This was done by the same Mary who sat at His feet, mesmerized by His words, in Luke 10:38–42. She was the sister of Martha and Lazarus, whom Jesus raised from the dead.

The timing of Mary's offering was just days before His death, and Jesus said she was anointing Him for His burial. Whether Mary had grasped the reality of His words about His imminent death and resurrection, or whether Jesus was simply accepting the offering in that light is unclear. Two things we do know: It was a very costly offering from Mary—and it was precious to the Lord. "Wherever this gospel is preached in the whole world, what this woman has done shall also be spoken of in memory of her," He stated (Matthew 26:13).

Who knows, maybe the fragrance lingering in His hair helped sustain Him as He agonized in Gethsemane. Perhaps the sweet aroma comforted Him through the torturous six hours on the cross.

Never underestimate the fragrance of worship.

Others in the room thought Mary's offering was a waste. Some scolded her. I know the feeling. When I cancelled all other activities for three months in our church in Colorado Springs, lavishing ninety days of 24/7 worship on the Lord, I, too, was criticized. One well-known Christian leader scolded me severely, calling the ninety days of worship "a complete waste of time."

It's fascinating how different people's perspectives can be. For me, those three months remain the best three months of my life. They were my alabaster box of costly perfume, the greatest offering I've had the pleasure of giving Christ. For the man who rebuked me, it was a complete waste of time. Never let the lack of revelation in others cheapen your offering. Don't water down your perfume, either, just to save a little money, or substitute your best "myrrh" with some cheap off brand. Give Him your best.

Others may mock your sacrifice of time, but go ahead and "waste" it on Him. Some will scold you, calling your passionate praise radical, but pour out your offering in spite of their ridicule. Still others will label your extravagant worship as excessive religious zeal. Don't let their misguided criticism deter you—pour out your costly perfume!

The list of Christ's followers in the room that day is almost mind-boggling. The twelve disciples were there. You'd think they would have understood the offering, but they were too practical: "It should have been given to the poor," was their protest. Christ's thoughts? "Go ahead and anoint Me and I'll be the offering for the poor."

Simon the leper (or should we say, "former leper"!) was present. They were actually in his home. You might think his new skin, replaced appendages, and restored life would merit the "wasting" of some costly perfume on Jesus. Evidently not. At least he didn't come to Mary's defense. And then there was Lazarus, Mary's brother, whom Jesus had raised from the dead. Surely he would see the validity of his sister's sacrifice. But no, he didn't come to her defense, either.

Could it be that the others' familiarity with Christ had lessened His worth? We don't know. We do know that only one worshiper that day had the fullness of revelation necessary to anoint the Savior. How sadly typical. Most miss the opportunity. It is not uncommon for me to see worshipers waste opportunities to break their alabaster box of love and pour it onto the Master. But they've been around Him so much, sang so many songs, and prayed so many prayers that the experience isn't worth quite what it used to be. So they give Him token praise and watered-down worship. Cheap perfume. I doubt if the fragrance makes it past Sunday lunch.

So while the others that day wasted an opportunity to comfort God, Mary "wasted" her perfume. Its fragrance sustained Him through the beatings, mocking, spittle, spikes, and thorns.

Don't allow another day to go by without becoming one of the "fragrance creators." Let nothing deter you. Your alabaster box is your heart, your love and worship the perfume. Break it open and pour it out. At the scent of your offering, He'll come. And He'll cherish yours, just as He did Mary's.

Prayer

Father, how great is this love that compels You to receive sinners laid down at Your feet. It's this extravagant love that led You to give the life of Your Son, Jesus, who now stands in my defense. Astounding!

As a drink offering, Jesus, You poured out Your life and made a way to the Father for me. And although Your gift is a matchless one, I want to be a laid-down lover all my days. May I never allow the opinions of others or concern for my reputation withhold my affections or deter my impassioned gaze toward You.

I thank You, Jesus, for receiving and cherishing my time, my talents, my devotion, and my heart as an alabaster jar of perfume. May I freely pour out every ounce of my life as a lavish display of adoration, an aroma that's pleasing to You.

I refuse to let the lack of revelation in others cheapen my offering. Jesus, You are worthy of the best. I break open my heart in passionate worship; never watered-down versions from me. At the end of my days may my epitaph read: "A life wasted on Jesus; a fragrance adorning the Bridegroom King."

(Prayer taken from: Ezekiel 20:41; Luke 7:37–38; Mark 14:3–9; Psalm 45:8; Song of Songs 1:12, Song of Songs 5:1, 5, 13; 2 Corinthians 2:14)

15

THE FRIENDSHIP

I called myself a Christian for seventeen years before I discovered I could have a truly personal relationship with God. Prior to this, I certainly knew Him as God and I definitely knew Him as my Savior. I didn't, however, know Him as my Father, and walking with Him as a friend wasn't even in the field of view. Satan and his team, with lots of help from religion, have painted God as a very distant, nonrelational being. If thought of at all, our Creator is primarily considered the Judge or, in times of crisis, a possible but unlikely means of help. Our adversary is nothing if not a very skilled deceiver.

The thought of friendship with God is more than simply intriguing to me. It messes with me! It tugs at my heart and calls out to me. Like the natal homing of a sea turtle experiencing the invisible but irresistible pull to the place of its birth, it woos me. Somehow I know in the deepest part of my nature that it is my destination, my home. His desire for friendship was the place in His heart where we were conceived. Our quest and destiny should be to find it again.

A few years ago I was elk hunting in the mountains of Colorado when I saw a monument to friendship. High on a mountain, near the edge where one of the most majestic views imaginable could be seen, was a plaque encased in a rock. Tears came to my eyes as I read the words carved into the plaque.

> In memory of my friend and hunting partner, [name], with whom I roamed these mountains from 1963–2003. He loved these mountains, streams, snow-packed peaks and beautiful valleys. I miss him.
>
> [Name]
> 1930–2003

It may sound overly dramatic, but I removed my hat and stood in silence, saluting the friendship enjoyed by these men. I tried to imagine the joys and memories created, as well as the pain of the loss he must have felt as an old warrior climbed this hill, memorial in hand, to honor the memory of a true friend. One can only imagine the hours they shared together. The only way to truly understand the camaraderie that develops when friends share the wonder and awe of creation together is to experience it. I thought of this as I stood looking over the vastness of the Rocky Mountains. Then I thought how much greater is the awesomeness of sharing moments such as these with the Creator Himself.

A friendship implies closeness and takes time to develop. It is comprised of trust, compatibility, affection, and, of course, a high level of interpersonal knowledge. I have many acquaintances but very few people I call my friends. The few I classify as such are those I enjoy spending quality time with, sharing life's experiences together. We're vulnerable with one another, freely communicating our hopes and dreams. I celebrate my victories with them and am comforted by them when I'm hurting. We keep it real. My walls are down when we're together; I'm unguarded and transparent, unafraid to let them see the real me—the unpolished version. I know they will always "be there" for me and I for them. Many more defining characteristics of friendship could be stated, but this much is clear: Friendship defines the highest level of relationship.

I'm sometimes amused when I hear the average Christian reference God as his or her "friend." There was a popular chorus a few years back about being God's friend. I liked the song, but as I listened to crowds singing it, I couldn't help but think how untrue it was for most of them. I suppose it's good to sing it as a reminder of God's offer to us, just as my parents used to sing "What a Friend We Have in Jesus." These songs may be reality for those who wrote them, but for the average person singing them, they simply aren't true. Most Christians have no true intimacy with God, spend very little time with Him, and have a very limited knowledge of His heart and ways. "A casual acquaintance" would best define their relationship with Him. We mustn't cheapen friendship by lowering the standard.

I want to quickly point out, however, that friendship with God is possible for every believer and is His desire for us. After Adam's fall, Abraham's walk with God was the first and probably the most in-depth revelation of this level of relationship. Three times in Scripture God called him His friend—and it's what He desires with each one of us. This is not only a part of our destiny, it's part of God's dream.

In exposing our shallow understanding of friendship with God and the fact that so few experience it, I don't mean to impugn our intentions and motives. The fact is, we're much like Abraham was at the beginning of his journey with the Lord. Most of us begin our walk with God just as he did—wanting the benefits He offers. We aren't terribly interested in His dreams; we probably aren't even consciously aware that He has any. But we are aware that He can help us with our dreams, so we cut deals with Him, talk to Him primarily on the basis of our needs, and remind Him that He is our Father—our source.[1]

In a sermon called "The Disciple's Prayer," Haddon Robinson tells the following story, which pictures the unenlightened and inappropriate beginning.

When our children were small, we played a game. I'd take some coins in my fist. They'd sit on my lap and work to get my fingers open. According to the international rules of finger opening, once the finger was open, it couldn't be closed again. They would work at it, until they got the pennies in my hand. They would jump down and run away, filled with glee and delight. Just kids. Just a game.

Sometimes when we come to God, we come for the pennies in his hand.

"Lord, I need a passing grade. Help me to study."

"Lord, I need a job."

"Lord, I need a car."

We reach for the pennies. Then we walk away.[2]

We're all so incurably human. We see God primarily as our Provider. Do we really know Him as a friend? No, not at the beginning of our journey. God understands this, however, and in His love and humility is willing to meet us where we are. "He first loved us," the Scriptures tell us (1 John 4:19), not the other way around. His love embraces us and makes us His child. And just as a natural child doesn't begin its relationship on a friendship level with Mom and Dad, our heavenly Father knows we won't with Him, either.

Most of us, when younger and in our parents' home, trusted them to provide for us. Appropriately so. But for most of us the day arrived when we wanted to be more than just a well-cared-for child. I know I did—I wanted to be my parents' friend. At that point I cared more about their happiness, well-being, and dreams than I did their money. I wanted to give to them more than I wanted to take from them. We no longer talked only about my happiness; we discussed things that interested them, as well. Over the years their faith had been transferred to me, and we dreamed together about making a difference for God. Our relationship had matured into a friendship.

The same was true of Abraham. He started his journey with God looking for lands, blessings, and greatness. He embraced the promise of a biological son through whom he would produce a great nation. But thankfully, the relationship grew. There were even some rough spots along the way. When God didn't provide the son He promised Abraham and Sarah in the way they expected, they demonstrated their lack of trust by choosing to have a son through Hagar, Sarah's maid.

Still, though Abraham demonstrated humanness, in the end he proved his trust in God had grown to a level few people ever attain. He was even willing to sacrifice Isaac, his long-awaited son, believing if he did so, God would raise Isaac from the dead. What trust!

The Lord so cherished His friendship with Abraham that, when Abraham died, He saw to it Abraham was buried at Hebron, which actually means "friendship." I can't help but believe that, like the hunting friend's mountaintop plaque, this was God's tribute to their friendship. Upon Abraham's arrival in heaven, I like to think perhaps Jehovah stood, got everyone's attention, and honored the old patriarch: "This is Abraham, my friend. We dreamed together, and enjoyed the pleasure of one another's company."

When God is looking for someone in His family He can be vulnerable with, a friend with whom He can share His hopes, dreams, and, yes, even His disappointments, I hope He feels He can look to me. And when my life is over and my body laid to rest, if it can be said that He and I were friends, I will have been a success.

Prayer

I am so grateful, Father, that friendship with You is Your deepest desire for us. Thank You, Jesus, for restoring friendship with God to every believer; fulfilling our destiny and the dream of God's heart.

Thank You for lovingly receiving my childlike interactions as genuine offerings from an immature heart. Still, Your love is so great that You meet me there and woo me tenderly toward the place of deep intimacy and trust. May I always respond to Your invitation such that the quest of my life becomes to find this place of true friendship and live undone before You.

God, when You are looking for someone in Your family You can be vulnerable with, a friend with whom You can share Your hopes, dreams, and, yes, even Your disappointments, I hope You feel You can look to me. And when my life is over and my body laid to rest, if it can be said that You and I were friends, I will have been a success.

(Prayer taken from: Romans 5:10; 1 John 4:19; James 2:23; Job 29:4; John 17:22; Proverbs 3:5–6; Psalm 37:4; Psalm 16:11)

16

THE STRETCH

As you know by now, I love nature and the outdoors. Sunrise, sunset, mountains, oceans, rivers, streams, trees—I just find God to be a pretty good artist. I also love to check out the animals. I've watched squirrels gather nuts, rabbits nibble leaves and veggies, and woodpeckers bang away at trees—how do they do that without rattling their brains out?! Have you ever watched a hummingbird up close—their wings go a gazillion times per second; or observed an eagle as it soars—their wings don't move! How did God think up all this stuff?

I love observing elk, and listening to them, as well. The sounds they make are fascinating. You've never heard all of nature's wonders until you've heard a bull elk bugle. When you hear this up close, it's one of the greatest rushes you could ever imagine. In mating season, you can actually call in a bull elk using calls that mimic the sounds of a cow elk in heat. Attracted like moths to a flame, they come running. When they approach, it is with tenacious and fierce determination. They grunt, bugle, and snort, both to alert the cow they're coming and to warn any other bulls in the area that this is their date—back off.

The bugling begins from hundreds of yards away and continues every few minutes as they approach. The first time I heard this, I became more "wired" with adrenaline with every bugle. I was convinced that the archangel Gabriel was coming through the woods with his trumpet. We were hidden in some brush and the expert caller was luring him in, ever closer. Finally, Mr. Elk was no more than ten yards away. Still unable to see us but knowing his "date" was close, he grunted, let out an ear-piercing bugle, slung some slobber (evidently, this is a turn-on for cow elk!), pawed the ground . . . and I made my peace with God! Talk about scary.

If you've never heard the bugle of a bull elk, put it on your bucket list.

Contrary to what you might think, an elk's eyesight is not that great. They rely mostly on their senses of smell and hearing. I was observing a small herd of these majestic creatures one evening just before dark. The wind was just right, blowing my scent away from them, and I had just enough cover between the herd and myself to creep within twenty yards or so. Eventually, just to see if I could do it, I crawled, very slowly, out into the open and watched them. They never saw me.

One of the things that intrigued me most was the twitching of their ears. Ever vigilant, each time they heard a sound, their ears would prick up in order to hear it even better. Whether eating, drinking, or taking a step, they were always diligent to listen for a potential threat—their lives depended on it. As I watched them, the pricking up of their ears reminded me of a word I had studied (I know, I have this thing for word studies; they make me want to bugle). I recalled that this was the literal meaning of one of the Hebrew words for "listening," *qashab*: "to prick up the ears like an animal coming to alertness." This live picture, painted by the elk, was indeed worth a thousand words.

One of the places *qashab* is used is in Proverbs 4:20–22, a fairly well-known passage of Scripture:

> My son, *give attention to* my words; incline your ear to my sayings. Do not let them depart from your sight; keep them in the midst of your heart. For they are life to those who find them and health to their whole body (italics mine).

My understanding of "giving attention to" the Lord's words went to a whole new level as I watched the ever-vigilant ears of the elk. *Always listen diligently for His voice, as though your life depends on it,* is what came to my mind. *No matter what else you happen to be doing, remain tuned in to Him.*

The number one way we "listen" to Him, of course, is through His written Word, the Scriptures. If we give them more than a casual look, He will communicate to us through them, revealing to us hidden treasures of wisdom and knowledge. The passage here in Proverbs calls these gems of truth "life" and "health" producers.

God also speaks to us in ways other than Scripture, however. Jesus said His sheep hear His voice (John 10:27). Of course, these messages must be judged by Scripture. Spending time with God through prayer, worship, and quiet meditation tunes in the soul and awakens the heart, enabling us to hear Him. Life is loud—make it quiet down once in a while. Everything else will scream for your attention, but not the Lord. The Holy Spirit refuses to shout above the clamor and dissonance created by other voices and activities. For those who have grown to love the pleasure of His company enough to make time for Him, however, the still small voice of the Holy Spirit becomes easily discernible.

Life gets fast. Too fast. *The Economist* contributor Dan Montano writes,

> Every morning in Africa, a gazelle wakes up. It knows it must run faster than the fastest lion or it will be killed. Every morning a lion wakes up. It knows it must outrun the slowest gazelle or it will starve to death. It doesn't matter whether you are a lion or a gazelle; when the sun comes up, you'd better be running.[1]

How true, and it's true of us, as well. It should describe the business world, however, not your devotional life. Speed has its place, and at times is necessary. But when listening for the Holy Spirit, listen slowly. He is patient but won't be trivialized by casual glances and cursory conversation. Like any lover, He wants to be valued.

Turn aside and listen for His voice. This is one of the meanings of the word "incline" (*natah*) in Proverbs 4:20. Moses saw a bush on fire while not being consumed, and decided to "turn aside" and see it (Exodus 3:3). When he did, the Lord spoke to Him. If we'll turn aside, He will speak to us, as well. But He won't speak until we are captivated enough to turn aside.

This word *natah* means "to stretch toward, as in craning the neck in order to see or hear better." The long-necked bird we call a crane provides the genesis for this colloquialism. "Stretch" your neck toward God in order to easily and clearly hear His sayings. Show Him worth; assign Him value; demonstrate interest in His words. If you do so, He will speak.

Interestingly, these same two words, *qashab* and *natah*, describe not only our listening to God but also His listening to us. He, too, pricks His ears and cranes His neck, listening for the voices of His kids. Like the attentive ears of a doting mother with her newborn baby, God is listening for the sounds and stirrings of His little ones. Malachi 3:16 tells us,

> Then those who feared the Lord spoke to one another, and the Lord *gave attention* and heard it, and a book

of remembrance was written before Him for those who fear the Lord and who esteem His name (italics mine).

"Gave attention" is *qashab*. God's attentive ears pricked up when a few of His kids began talking about Him, and He was blessed by it. "Make a note of this," He told one of His assistants.

Religion or misinformed people may have sold you a bill of goods about God being distant, but don't believe it. Not only is He everlasting He is also *ever-listening*.

In Psalm 40:1, David says of the Lord, "I waited patiently for the Lord; And He *inclined* to me and heard my cry" (italics mine). "Inclined" is *natah*, God craning His neck, stretching it toward the cry of David. The entire Psalm is wonderful, but the verses immediately following describe a portion of David's overwhelming response to the Lord's favor and mercy.

> He brought me up out of the pit of destruction,
>   out of the miry clay,
> And He set my feet upon a rock making my
>   footsteps firm.
> He put a new song in my mouth, a song of
>   praise to our God;
> Many will see and fear and will trust in the Lord.
>
> How blessed is the man who has made the Lord
>   his trust,
> And has not turned to the proud, nor to those
>   who lapse into falsehood.

Many, O Lord my God, are the wonders which
    You have done,
And Your thoughts toward us; there is none to
    compare with You.
If I would declare and speak of them,
They would be too numerous to count.

Psalm 40:2–5

"Too numerous to count" is the phrase David used to describe our Father's thoughts toward us. He loves us, and as we turn aside to Him, He turns aside to us. The resulting face-to-face encounter is one of life's greatest pleasures. Don't allow a feverish pace and clamorous noises to rob you. Slow down and listen.

Prayer

Thank You, Father, for being the God that is ever-listening to every utterance from the hearts of Your kids. From Your throne of glory, You incline to hear my voice and attend to my prayers. How amazing this is!

Let the sounds that You hear from my life be so pleasing, that in heaven's book of remembrance some notations would reference my name, detailing all the ways in which I lavished love upon You and highly esteemed Your Name.

Lord, I want to hear Your voice speaking, and joyfully respond to the stirrings of Your beautiful heart. May I earnestly stretch my heart toward You—listening—giving attention to Your every word. Draw me to the hidden treasures that are found in the pages of Your Book. Wisdom, knowledge, life, and health to me, the Scriptures are my daily bread.

I don't want to be a casual listener, but wait on You and still my heart to hear, diligently stretching to lend my attention and ascribe to Your worth to Your words. May I turn aside frequently as a sheep who discerns well and faithfully follows the sound of the Shepherd's voice. I am listening . . .

(Prayer taken from: Psalm 40:1, Psalm 66:19; Malachi 3:16; Proverbs 2:1–2, Proverbs 5:1, Proverbs 4:20–22; John 10:27; Exodus 3:3)

17

THE UNDISTRACTED

I like football. Okay, I love football. And for all the NFL fans out there, the Dallas Cowboys may be America's team, but as any true fan knows, the Denver Broncos are God's team. That's why He made the sky blue and sunsets orange.

Several years ago when my younger daughter, Hannah, was only three or four, I was enjoying a great Broncos playoff game. Did you catch that? Not just a game—a *Broncos playoff* game. I had a great fire in the fireplace, had kicked back in my football recliner, and was into a great game. Hannah had no understanding of football and couldn't have cared less about the game.

She plopped down in my lap and, as girls do, began jabbering about something. She wasn't talking about anything terribly important—at least I didn't think it was all that important. But I was listening. Sort of. I was actually dividing my attention between her commentary and the exploits of John Elway. *This is real devotion to my daughter*, I thought. *Sharing my football time with her childish jabbering. Bronco's playoff football, at that. What a great dad I am.*

I was doing the typical distracted listening routine, an "uh-huh" here, an "ohhh" there, with a smile or two and a head nod thrown in for added effect. Sure, I was missing a play here or there, but, hey, that's just the price of *devotion*.

Hannah has always been very perceptive. And, of course, she has the particular female trait of wanting the men in her life to really listen. I don't know when that particular gene kicks in for women, but it obviously comes alive at an earlier age than I thought. After a few minutes of my divided attention, Hannah had finally had enough.

"Dad," she said rather sternly, as she placed one index finger on each cheek and turned my face directly toward her. "Look me in the eye and listen."

Women are taught these things at a young age!

I looked her in the eye and listened. That, my friend, is *undistracted* devotion.

Paul uses these two words, "undistracted devotion," in 1 Corinthians 7:35, speaking of our commitment to the Lord. The phrase actually comes from one Greek word, *euprosedros*. *Prosedros* by itself means "to sit forward or toward" someone or something. Imagine a person sitting in the presence of someone they are completely devoted to, leaning toward them in order to hear every word. Again, the prefix *eu* means "well," intensifying the concept to mean "sitting well toward"; thus, the translation "undistracted devotion." In our culture today we often use a similar phrase, "sitting on the edge of our seats." Obviously, we mean by this that we are fully captivated by someone or something.

Hannah wanted me to "sit well toward" her, giving her some face time. She needed to know that she, not the Broncos, was number one. And she was. At that moment my favorite color wasn't orange; it was brown, the color of her eyes.

God would like some face time with you. He knows you're busy and can't live like a monk, giving yourself to nonstop worship and meditation. He's also aware that you have a family to care for, work to perform, and the need for sleep. He doesn't want all of your time; He does, however, want some *undistracted* time. It's a matter of having the right priorities.

Bill Cowher is another great football fan. He's actually more than a fan, he was also a player and a coach. Cowher coached the Pittsburgh Steelers from 1992 through 2006, winning the Super Bowl for the '05–'06 season. He is presently an analyst on *The NFL Today*, aired by CBS.

Two things that made Cowher so successful were his focus and his intensity. Not surprisingly, the two together made him intensely focused. We football fans loved watching the Steelers games just to see the intense looks he gave players and officials. Huge, rock-hard linebackers would wilt under the intense glare of a Cowher stare.

But Cowher was also focused on his family. In *Sports Illustrated,* Tim Crothers wrote of him:

After almost every game, every practice . . . Cowher drives straight home to his wife, Kaye, and their three daughters. He doesn't do ads for Fords or frozen yogurt. He exists inside his two passions, family and football, exclusive of everything else.

He is so focused that one afternoon he was seated next to a woman at a civic luncheon and politely asked, "What is it you do?" The woman responded, "I'm the mayor of Pittsburgh."[1]

Granted, it's a good idea to know who your mayor is, but Cowher shows us an essential truth: You can't focus on everything. We must focus on the things that matter most.

I have found that priorities are heart related. What means most to me is what I'll most likely prioritize. If we find ourselves uninterested in the pleasure of God's company, the place to start is with repentance. We should ask God to forgive us of indifference toward Him, and to awaken passion in us. Then begin spending quality time with Him. As we do, hunger for His presence will increase and we will look forward to those times.

As King Solomon was about to begin his reign over Israel, he prayed a prayer God couldn't resist. "So give

Your servant an understanding heart to judge Your people to discern between good and evil. For who is able to judge this great people of Yours?" (1 Kings 3:9). The phrase "an understanding heart" should actually be translated "a hearing heart." The translators struggle with a "hearing" heart, so they don't word it this way. But the Hebrew word is *shama*, and it does mean "to hear." Solomon asked for a hearing heart.

Hearts can hear, but only when they're undistracted. In times past, before we had refrigerators, people used icehouses to preserve food. They had thick walls and were well insulated. In winter, large chunks of ice were taken from lakes, ponds, or streams and laid on the floor, then covered with a thick layer of sawdust to insulate it. This made a great "refrigerator."

One day a gentleman lost an expensive watch in the icehouse. Due to the thickness of the sawdust, all efforts to find it failed. Others looked, also in vain. Finally, a small boy slipped into the icehouse when no one was around and promptly found the valuable watch.

Surprised, the men asked the young boy how he had so easily and quickly found the valuable timepiece.

"I closed the door, lay down on the floor, and was very quiet," replied the lad. "Pretty soon I heard it ticking."[2]

The problem isn't God's refusal to speak but our refusal or inability to get quiet enough to hear. Silencing the soul is a learned art. The psalmist David spoke of this. "Surely I have composed and quieted my soul; like a weaned child rests against his mother" (Psalm

131:2). When we quiet the soul, we can hear His voice in our hearts.

Several years ago I was preparing to speak at a conference in Canada. As I spoke with the Lord about the service, I heard Him speak. It wasn't loud, and it certainly wasn't audible. It was a gentle voice in my heart, almost like the ticking of a watch: *"Japan is heavy on my heart today."*

I was surprised. I knew it was God—I certainly wasn't thinking about Japan—but the way He said it surprised me. It had never occurred to me that a particular place might be on God's heart more than others at a given time. I suppose I just assumed every place was equally on God's heart all the time.

"I must have a breakthrough there," He continued. "Rather than speak in your session today, would you give the time to prayer for a breakthrough in Japan?"

I was stunned. God didn't *demand* that I do this; He *asked* if I would! It was almost as if I was hearing the longing of His heart, not words from His mouth. I was deeply moved that He would allow me into His thoughts.

"Of course I will, Lord," was my quick and heartfelt response.

As I shared with the gathering what I had heard, several dozen people in the audience began to chatter. They shouted from their seats that they were from Japan! We invited them to the ministry area up front and prayed for them and for their nation. It was a very special time.

The conference attendees were still praying for them an hour later when I left for the airport. A few weeks after this I received an email from someone in Japan thanking me for this time of intercession. Someone had taken a recording of the session to Japan, and it was circulated throughout many Japanese churches. The email spoke of the great encouragement the prayers provided and testified to the breakthroughs they had received since then. God is amazing.

And He still speaks to those who will listen.

Slow down a little and let God into your world. If you do, He'll allow you into His. He will find the pleasure of your undistracted devotion, and you will experience the pleasure of hearing His heart.

Look Him in the eyes and listen.

Prayer

Father, I thank You for Your undivided attentiveness toward me. It's astonishing to know that You are ravished by just one glance from my eye. What pleasures are provoked within Your heart when I choose not just to glance, but to gaze?

In repentance I sit before You today, for letting myself lose interest in the pleasure of Your company. Forgive me for my indifference, awaken passion for Your presence, and guide me in resetting my priorities.

Holy Spirit, teach me the art of waiting with an undivided heart so that my hunger for Your presence will increase. You are worthy of my undistracted devotion, where I sit at the edge of my seat, watching and listening intently for every move, every word that You speak.

Like Solomon, I ask, would You grant unto me a hearing heart that can quiet itself enough to hear the longings of Your heart? What a beautiful and rewarding exchange. Jesus, I'm slowing down to look into Your eyes and to listen . . .

(Prayer taken from: Song of Solomon 4:9; Matthew 13:15; 1 Corinthians 7:35; Isaiah 50:7; 1 Kings 3:9, 28; 1 Kings 10:24; Psalm 131:2)

18

THE COURTSHIP

I remember when Ceci and I were courting. I was fairly indifferent toward her at first—she had to do the pursuing. NOT. I proposed to her after only a week of dating. I think it would be fair to say I was smitten. Her big brown eyes, long dark hair, and overall beauty knocked me off my feet.

Though it only took me a week to propose to her, we did wait nine months before tying the knot. Those were the longest nine months of my life. I wanted to be with her all the time. Both of us were Bible school students, and over the summer I went back to Ohio while she went on tour with the school's choir. That three-month separation felt like ten years!

It's fair to say that during our courtship nothing mattered more to me than spending time with Ceci.

It seemed that every time we were together I learned something new about her and grew to love her more. I wanted more than anything to please her and make her happy. Our courtship was awesome—even our time apart strengthened our love.

As foreign as the concept may seem, the Scriptures speak of our "courting" God. Proverbs 3:5–6 tells us, "Trust in the Lord with all your heart, and do not lean on your own understanding. In all your ways acknowledge Him, and He will make your paths straight."

In this familiar passage, "ways" is from the Hebrew word *derek*, which refers to a journey, a course of life, or a mode of action. It is used in various contexts, including courting. Imagine that; we can court God. On life's journey, we will court many things: success, advancements, fame, other people, money, favor, and a myriad of other things. Seeking and loving God with all of our heart, soul, mind, and strength is often lost in the melee. Gordon Dahl aptly said, "Most middle-class Americans tend to worship their work, to work at their play, and to play at their worship."[1] How true, and nothing is more lethal to our spiritual life. We need to court God every day. Sometimes I feel like the small child in *The Family Circus* cartoon who ran up to his mother exclaiming, "I need a hug, Mommy. I used up the last one."[2] It doesn't take long to use up our spiritual hugs.

In the same passage, "acknowledge" is from the Hebrew word *yada*, which means "to know someone intimately." It is actually used of a man and woman knowing one another sexually. Courting God in all of our ways (*derek*) leads to intimacy (*yada*), which leads to spiritual conception. Just as Adam "knew" Eve and she conceived, we can know God in ways that allow Him to speak to us. When He speaks, His word becomes a seed in our hearts (see 1 Peter 1:23), and that which is born from our lives is now of Him, not just from our own mind. Our visions, plans, methods, ministries, relationships—all of these can then be the offspring of the Holy Spirit, not just of ourselves.

God isn't into surrogate parenting—someone else carrying His seed of revelation for us. He wants to sow it into us *personally*, breathing His word into our hearts. Insights we receive from others through sermons and books are good and valid, but if that is the only way we receive spiritual insight, we're living far below our privileges.

God is not into artificial insemination, either—placing His seed in us without an intimate relationship. CDs, seminars, and books are all good, but they must not take the place of hearing from Him *personally* and *directly*. Conferences where the word of God is flowing wonderfully can become nothing more than a sterile laboratory of information if we're not careful. Frankly, I believe many Sunday morning services also fit this description. Shared ideas are good, and reinventing the wheel isn't necessary, but that doesn't negate our need for fresh revelation. We must not be satisfied only with another's.

The problem, of course, is not in receiving teaching through someone else; this is obviously one of the ways God speaks to us. Our problem is when this becomes the primary source of our information. We cannot live only on another person's revelation. We must hear from God ourselves. And when He does speak to us through someone else, we still should pray and meditate over the information (courting God), which moves it from the mind to the heart and makes it now a personal word of revelation to us.

As strange as it may sound, we can even become "pregnant" with someone else's revelation and "birth" another person's child! The body of Christ, especially in churches, is filled with people trying to walk in someone else's revelation, vision, ideas, and methods. And we often wonder why so much of what we attempt in trying to reach people for Christ produces so little fruit. Every time I see another church-growth conference advertised, I cringe. It isn't that the principles shared are wrong. They probably worked well for the person sharing them. But each of us still must allow the Holy Spirit to show us how and apply the principles to our personal lives and ministries. The method that worked for one may not work for another; principles can be applied many ways and at many times.[3]

The apostle Paul understood the need for this personal walk with God. Paul was still "courting" Him at the end of His life and ministry. He stated,

But whatever things were gain to me, those things I have counted as loss for the sake of Christ. More than that, I count all things to be loss in view of the surpassing value of *knowing* Christ Jesus my Lord, for whom I have suffered the loss of all things, and count them but rubbish so that I may gain Christ. . . . That I may *know* Him and the power of His resurrection.

Philippians 3:7–8, 10, italics mine

The word Paul used for "knowing" God, *ginosko*, is similar to *yada*. It, too, is a *relational* knowledge. Like *yada*, it is used in reference to a man and woman knowing one another physically. Mary asked the angel Gabriel how she could have a child since she had never "known" (*ginosko*) a man (Luke 1:34). Paul was saying He had forsaken all other "lovers" in his courting of God. He wanted to know Him intimately.

Ginosko also carries the meaning of a *progressive* or *growing* knowledge. In the same way a husband and wife's knowledge of one another should increase over time, enhancing their relationship, Paul was stating that he wanted to know Christ even more intimately. By this time in Paul's life, He had been taken to heaven, where he was given sufficient revelation to write much of the New Testament. He actually saw God in person! Yet, incredibly, he was still saying he wanted to know Him more. You'll never exhaust the depths of God. The pleasure of His company makes you want the pleasure of His company!

Finally, not only is *ginosko* relational and progressive, it is an "effectional" knowledge, having an effect on the knower. The more we see God, the more we become like Him. Second Corinthians 3:18 tells us, "But we all, with unveiled face, beholding as in a mirror the glory of the Lord, are being transformed into the same image from glory to glory, just as from the Lord, the Spirit." God's personhood is so powerful that as we gaze upon Him, His very image is burned into us like light on a negative. We are transformed back into His image and likeness, which we lost at Adam's fall.

In his book *Good Morning, Merry Sunshine*, *Chicago Tribune* columnist Bob Greene chronicles his infant daughter's first year of life. When little Amanda began crawling, he records:

> This is something I'm having trouble getting used to. I will be in bed reading a book or watching TV. And I will look down at the foot of the bed and there will be Amanda's head staring back at me.
>
> Apparently I've become one of the objects that fascinate her. . . . It's so strange. After months of having to go to her, now she is choosing to come to me. I don't know quite how to react. All I can figure is that she likes the idea of coming in and looking at me. She doesn't expect anything in return. I'll return her gaze and in a few minutes she'll decide she wants to be back in the living room and off she'll crawl again.[4]

Take some time to stare at Papa God. I promise you He'll gaze back, straight in the eye. Words aren't always needed. I've spent hours conversing with God without saying a word. Hearts don't always need words to communicate; they just need to be together.

Prayer

I stand amazed, God, as I reflect upon the beautiful romance that we share. You court me with kindness, wooing my heart, then patiently await my response. I in turn can court You, my Lord, and this is where I'm in awe. The Almighty God of Creation is moved by the simplest love-gestures from my heart.

Jesus, I want my knowledge of You to be progressive, knowing Your heart more and more—intimately acquainted with Your dreams and desires, and letting them become my own. Impregnate me with Your seeds of revelation concerning Your purposes and plans, Your will and ways. Let me give birth to Your dreams breathed upon my heart.

May I never be satisfied with accessing through another what is readily available to me. Holy Spirit, guide me in the art of courting God, discovering new facets of Your heart—the heights, depths, widths, lengths of Your love.

May my heart ever echo this cry: All things pale in comparison to the surpassing greatness of knowing Christ Jesus my Lord—both Your power and Your suffering, the resurrection and the cross. I want to see and reflect Your glory. I will forsake other lovers to gaze into Your eyes and experience the great pleasure of Your company.

(Prayer taken from: Proverbs 3:5–6; 1 Peter 1:23; Luke 8:11; Philippians 3:7–10; Psalm 73:25; John 17:3; 2 Peter 1: 2–3; 2 Corinthians 3:18; John 17:24)

19

THE LISTENER

I grew up believing I was ugly. With my movie-star good looks, I know this seems unbelievable, but it's true. Because of this, meeting and conversing with people was difficult for me; I became introverted, insecure, and shy.

This intensified when I was ten years old. My Sunday school class had a Scripture memorization program, and at the end of it we were scheduled to quote our verses in front of the congregation on a Sunday morning. When my turn came, I couldn't remember my verse. Panic set in, which only made it worse, and my mind went completely blank. I doubt if I could have spelled my name.

The pastor was sitting on the front row, and rather than encourage me and prompt me a little, he lost patience. This, of course, made my problem worse. In complete embarrassment and humiliation, I began to cry. This angered him even more, and with disgust, he told me to go sit down. That pastor was my dad.

Dad had insecurity issues of his own, and I have always assumed that my failure embarrassed him. Then my weakness (crying) angered him. I never want to dishonor his memory. He tried his best to be a good father, and I know he loved me. In spite of his failures and weaknesses, I loved him, as well. The last twenty years or more of his life he modeled for me a walk with God worth emulating.

Nevertheless, this experience scarred me in a horrible way. From that moment forward I couldn't speak in front of people. One-on-one I could function, but any time I was in front of a group—whether it was a class at school or in a youth group—my mind would go blank and I was finished. Eventually, I stopped even trying. I preferred receiving an F on an oral book report than trying to give it. It was a paralyzing fear.

I remember dropping a course in college because of a "name game" the teacher had us play in our first class. Starting at the front, each student had to stand and tell their name, then repeat all the names of everyone before them. By the time they came to me, there were probably fifteen to twenty names to recite. I stood and told them my name, and then, as usual, my mind went blank. I sat down, deeply embarrassed and humiliated; when class ended I went to the appropriate office and dropped the course.

Fear—whether of the dark, of failing, or of rejection—is a tormenting and paralyzing thing. Thankfully, I have been freed from my fear of public speaking. But for years, having experienced such a debilitating fear, I had difficulty embracing Scriptures that spoke positively of "the fear of the Lord." *Why would anyone want a relationship with someone they had to be afraid of?* I wondered. And though I didn't embrace the concept, I actually *was* afraid of God.

It certainly is not possible to enjoy God if you're afraid of Him. I do not ever remember enjoying the pleasure of His company for the first nineteen years of my life, even though I was definitely born again. My relationship with Him can be described by the boyhood experience of T. H. White:

> My father made me a wooden castle big enough to get into, and he fixed real pistol barrels beneath its battlements to fire a salute on my birthday but made me sit in front the first night . . . to receive the salute, and I, believing I was to be shot, cried.[1]

That pretty much sums up my early concept of God. He was looking for any reason to shoot me. As far as I was concerned, He was makin' a list, checkin' it twice, to see if I'd been naughty or nice. And if I was less than perfect, there would be hell to pay—literally. The fear of the Lord was anything but appealing to me. In fact, like most people I believed the devil wanted me to have fun; God, the serious and stern Judge that He was, wanted me to be sober-minded and live a boring life. How horribly inaccurate. Thankfully, my perception of Him has changed and I now believe wholeheartedly in His goodness.

I have since discovered that my concept of "the fear of the Lord" was distorted. Several different Hebrew and Greek words in Scripture are translated as "fear." Some of them are good fears, some not. *Phobos*, for example, is a dread or terror. Our English word *phobia* originates from this word. Scripture makes it clear that God doesn't want us to experience this type of fear. "There is no fear in love; but perfect love casts out fear, because fear involves punishment, and the one who fears is not perfected in love" (1 John 4:18).

There is also the word *deilia*, which is a timidity or cowardice type of fear. As a young boy I had become *deilia* through my insecurities. This, and the trauma I experienced when publically humiliated, led to a *phobos* of speaking in front of people. But God says in 2 Timothy 1:7, "For God has not given us a spirit of timidity (*deilia*), but of power and love and discipline." Our heavenly Father doesn't want us to be timid or insecure. Like any good parent, He wants us secure, especially in our relationship with Him. Father God doesn't operate like the typical drill sergeant with his recruits, whipping us into shape through fear and intimidation. That may be appropriate for soldiers, but not kids.

What type of fear, then, are we to have toward the Lord? The Greek word is *eulabeia*, which is a reverence or piety; it is an awe, an overwhelming feeling of wonder, admiration, or respect. Jesus actually possessed this type of fear toward His Father, God, though He certainly was never afraid of Him:

> In the days of His flesh, He offered up both prayers and supplications with loud crying and tears to the One able to save Him from death, and He was heard because of His piety (*eulabeia*).
>
> Hebrews 5:7

Possessing a respect and awe of God brings great reward to us. It is spoken of as the beginning of knowledge (Proverbs 1:7). It is also used to describe the respect Abraham had for God, which enabled him to trust the Lord even with his son Isaac's life (Genesis 22:12). It is somewhat ironic that a "fear" engendered faith, but it did. Abraham's respect of God caused him to believe fully in His goodness, and that He was trustworthy. This is also the type of respect we are instructed to have for our parents, which carries with it the promise of a long life (Leviticus 19:3).

There's a revealing description in the book of Malachi of how this type of honor blesses the Lord. The context of this book is the unfaithfulness of Israel, a people God loved very much and who were supposed to be walking in covenant with Him. They had turned away from Him, however, and were instead worshiping idols. God's desire was for them to return to Him, and He was using Malachi to challenge them accordingly.

In the midst of this season in which God was experiencing such painful rejection, several individuals who still honored and respected Him were conversing. Based on the passage, their conversation was obviously honoring toward Him. As they were speaking to one another, the Lord heard it and was deeply moved.

> Then those who feared the Lord spoke to one another, and the Lord *gave attention* and heard it, and a book of remembrance was written before Him for those who fear the Lord and who esteem His name. "And they will be Mine," says the Lord of hosts, "on the day that I prepare My own possession, and I will spare them as a man spares his own son who serves him. So you will again distinguish between the righteous and the wicked, between one who serves God and one who does not serve Him."
>
> Malachi 3:16–18, italics mine

"Gave attention" is from the Hebrew word *qashab*. We have already defined this word as meaning "to prick up the ears, like an animal coming to alertness." Imagine God, feeling the pain of unfaithfulness and broken relationships, suddenly hearing some of His family speaking of Him with respectful and loving terminology. He became alert and began listening to them attentively. This is what happened here in Malachi.

God is always alert for the sounds of love. John said He is love personified (1 John 4:8, 16), and as our loving Father and friend, He enjoys the company of those who also honor the relationship.

The passage in Malachi goes on to say the Lord "heard" these individuals. Among other definitions, this Hebrew word also means "to eavesdrop." God began eavesdropping on their conversation, not to catch them doing something wrong but because their conversation was blessing Him!

Ironically, I'm in a coffee shop as I am writing this, and the two young ladies at the table next to me are proving my point. Seeing my open Bible in front of me prompted a discussion between them concerning God, church, and religion. They don't like the church, seeing most Christians as judgmental and hypocritical. (Do you think perhaps they want me to hear them?) And their concept of God is anything but the relational friend and Father He is. Sadly, it sounds like religiosity is all they've ever been exposed to.

How tragic but sadly common. God's heart is so incredibly misunderstood. Jesus, who came to show us the true nature of God, was so kind He was loved by young and old, including sinners. Only self-righteous, religious legalists and the truly evil didn't like Him. He was interesting, compassionate, and kind.

In Malachi's day, God's heart was so moved by these people who loved and honored Him that He instructed angels to create "a book of remembrance" and record their names in it. He would honor them later. He called them "mine" and His "possession" (*segullah*). *Segullah* was the word for a treasure or jewel. The Lord was so deeply moved by what He was hearing, He referred to these friends as a treasure to His heart.

Amazing.

You, too, can be a treasure to Him. It won't be because you perform well enough, but because you respect and honor Him. He is listening, not to catch you in a failure so He can shout at you, but to enjoy your company. In the midst of all the rebellion and idolatry on the planet, give Him some love.

Talk to Him. Today.

Prayer

Father, I am so grateful for Your Son, Jesus—the love of the Father fully expressed. Jesus, You are perfect love personified; You drive away all my fears, You complete me and redefine my worldview. Knowing You, Jesus, I can wholeheartedly believe in the Father's goodness and draw near in reverent awe.

May I walk only in the fear that results in the highest honor, admiration, and respect for God. Let me reap the rewards of walking in the fear of the Lord; wisdom and revelation, knowledge and faith, and a trust in God that is constant and strong.

I pray that Your listening ears, today, God, would be drawn to the sounds of endearment toward You from my heart. Let it be such that the heavenly hosts record my name as a treasured lover of God.

(Prayer taken from: 1 John 4:18; 1 John 5:8, 16; 2 Timothy 1:7; Hebrews 5:7; Proverbs 1:7; Malachi 3:16–18)

20

The Lingerers

When I was a student at Christ For The Nations Institute thirty-five years ago—back when I could run for miles and still had a six-pack, all my hair, and no wrinkles—I was diligent to spend quality amounts of time every day with God. I had actually developed this lifestyle prior to attending CFNI. Before work each day I'd wake up an hour or more earlier than necessary in order to spend time praying and reading the Word. I loved hanging out with God then, and still do.

My practice while a student was to pray and/or spend time reading Scripture for at least an hour before school began with chapel at 8:00 a.m. Chapel didn't consist of a message but was thirty-five minutes of glorious worship. (We still begin each day this way at CFNI, building our lives around the Lord's presence.) Combining these two things meant that I had a good hour and a half at the beginning of every day to enjoy the pleasure of His company.

Many days I would also pray another thirty to forty-five minutes after our last class ended at noon. I would then rush to the cafeteria before it closed at 1:00 p.m. During these forty-five minutes I would pray and meditate over what I had learned that day, as well as anything the Holy Spirit would bring to my mind to intercede for. These times of lingering became special to me, and I believe they were to the Lord, as well. I mention this two-plus hours per day I spent with the Lord not to boast but to emphasize the fact that anyone can develop a love for His presence. I was anything but a spiritual giant at this time of my life, only very hungry for God.

One afternoon at my usual 12:45 time, I came down from the balcony, where I often spent this last forty-five minutes with the Lord. The student council was selling tickets for a banquet, and they were just putting their supplies away, preparing to leave. Two of them, a guy and a girl, were carrying a folding table to a closet. The girl, whom I had never met, was the most beautiful girl I had ever seen.

I decided right then to marry her!

I quickly grabbed her end of the table, demonstrating my chivalry and muscle. The student council member on the other end of the table, whom I knew, introduced us. It took me a few weeks to get the nerve to ask her out, but when I did she quickly said yes. She, too, was smitten. Ceci and I were married nine months later.

That, my friend, is what happens when you linger with God!

Okay, you may not be rewarded with a spouse, but good things do happen to "lingerers." I've always believed God orchestrated the timing of our meeting just to demonstrate how much He enjoyed our times together. It would be just like Him to do so—He is a rewarder of those who diligently seek Him (Hebrews 11:6). Of course, the greatest reward is simply the privilege of connecting with Him.

One definition of *linger* is "to leave slowly and hesitantly." If you don't find yourself leaving God's presence slowly and hesitantly, there's a short somewhere in the connection. When you truly connect with Him, it's like a warm bed on a wintery morning—you don't want to leave it. Regular visitors to the throne of grace become lingerers, pure and simple.

Charles Swindoll shares this story:

I vividly remember some time back being caught in the undertow of too many commitments in too few days. It wasn't long before I was snapping at my wife and our children, choking down my food at mealtimes, and feeling irritated at those unexpected interruptions through the day. Before long, things around our home started reflecting the pattern of my hurry-up style. It was becoming unbearable. I distinctly recall after supper one evening the words of our younger daughter,

Colleen. She wanted to tell me something important that had happened to her at school that day. She hurriedly began, "Daddy, I wanna tell you somethin' andIwillltellyoureallyfast."

Suddenly realizing her frustration, I answered, "Honey, you can tell me . . . and you don't have to tell me really fast. Say it slowly."

I'll never forget her answer: "Then *listen* slowly."[1]

You'll never find yourself having to say to your heavenly Father, "Then listen slowly." He has plenty of time for you and loves it when you linger in His presence. In fact, His biggest problem is our *limited* time with Him, not our lingering. We're often in such a hurry we actually *want* Him to listen really fast. But He isn't our spiritual Santa Claus, wanting us to take our two minutes in His lap, give Him our wish list, and be on our way. He is Abba-Papa.

Our Father is not easily offended. He is patient and longsuffering, and His loving-kindness is everlasting. But still, I can't help but wonder if He doesn't get offended at the way we treat Him. We give Him such little time, expecting Him to listen fast and perform quickly. I have a friend who actually believes the Lord once told him, "Don't defile My presence with your impatience."

Ouch.

David, the shepherd and psalmist who became king over Israel, was a lingerer; he loved being in God's presence and he left slowly and hesitantly. David once said, "One thing I have asked from the Lord, that I shall seek:

that I may dwell in the house of the Lord all the days of my life, to behold the beauty of the Lord and to meditate in His temple" (Psalm 27:4). Notice the words *dwell*, *behold*, and *meditate*. Those are lingering terms. He also said, "O Lord, I love the habitation of Your house and the place where Your glory dwells" (Psalm 26:8). You don't make statements like that unless you've learned to linger.

First we *learn* to linger, then He becomes addictive and we *love* to linger. Listen to David's language: "I *love* the habitation of Your house." I enjoy reading about David and his walk with God. It has been revealing and enriching to observe their relationship in the Scriptures—the good, the bad, and the ugly. One thing I especially like is that David kept it real, sharing with God his most intimate thoughts. Whether he was joyful, discouraged, lonely, or on top of the world, David talked to the Lord about it. He knew God wanted to be involved in his world, and he wanted to be in God's.

Eventually, a change came in their relationship, a change so subtle that most people never think about it. Many people love God's presence. Thankfully, the worship movement of the last thirty to forty years has taught many of us the difference between singing and worshiping. And as we have learned to truly worship, we've discovered the glorious truth that it attracts His very presence (Psalm 22:3). Through this process, we've come to expect and enjoy the presence of the Lord.

David understood this and was a passionate lover of God's presence. As much as he loved the Lord's presence, however, David was never called "a man after God's *presence*." He had the awe-inspiring honor of being referred to by the Lord as "a man after My *heart*" (see Acts 13:22, italics mine). There can be a huge difference between pursuing God's heart and experiencing His presence.

It is possible to be in a person's presence and never make it into their heart. There are plenty of people I'm willing to hang out with, but very few I'll allow into my heart. That part of me is reserved for the people I've spent enough time with to know I can trust their motives and intentions. I need to be confident my heart has value to them. It is breakable; I want it handled with care.

God is no different. His heart can be broken. His emotions can be wounded and His hopes dashed. He allows many into His presence but is much more selective with His heart. His presence is free, but His heart will cost you time and effort. But oh, how worth the effort He is. Pay the price to find His heart, no matter what it costs you!

I emphasize this to my students at Christ For The Nations Institute, that when considering their futures, not to focus first on a vision or dream. So often young people are challenged to dream big, to develop a large vision. Personally, I've discovered how easy it is for my own ambition and selfish desires to sneak into my plans when I begin with the dream itself. I urge the students to seek God's *heart*, not a dream. When they find His heart, hidden inside they'll also discover their purpose and destiny. Then they can dream, knowing it's God's dream for their life.

Sadly, you may not encounter much competition on this quest for God's heart. Many love His presence and are willing to sing a few songs once or twice a week to enter it. Few, however, are after His heart. Choose to become one who is. Don't settle for a cursory look; be a lingerer.

Talk to Him slowly, listen to Him slowly, and leave Him slowly.

Prayer

Father, You are worthy of my time and attention, of the greatest affections of my heart. You are generously kind in rewarding those who diligently seek You with greater glimpses of the beauty of Your heart.

Forgive me for my impatience, my Lord, when approaching Your throne of grace. Like Joshua at the Tent of Meeting, I want to be one who loves to linger in Your presence, leaving slowly and hesitantly. Father, this one thing I ask for and seek: to dwell in Your house all my days, beholding Your beauty and meditating upon Your Word. Lingering . . . lingering . . .

I want to go further still than enjoying the glorious place where You dwell. I love to enjoy the pleasures of Your presence, but I want also to seek after Your heart. I know there's a high price that must be paid to enter that most intimate place, but time and effort I'm determined to give to find and know Your heart. I will linger, longer still . . .

(Prayer taken from: Hebrews 11:6; Exodus 33:11; Psalm 27:4, Psalm 26:8, Psalm 22:3; Acts 13:22)

21

THE VISIT

I watched the cesarean-section delivery of a baby on television once. It was on one of those educational channels that enlighten us to some of the things we need to know to survive in life. Thank God for satellite TV!

I also saw a face-lift on the same channel. They peeled the skin right off the face! Believe me, now I know why they say beauty is only skin deep! Then they sucked up a bunch of cellulite. I don't know what kind of cells those are, but they also sucked up some fat—I knew what that was. Seemed to me they should have left the "lite" cells and sucked up the fat cells, but I reckon they had some reason for doing what they did. The things we do to look better.

The delivery of the baby fascinated me most. I always figured they just cut the skin and out plopped the baby. No way! They pert-near (that's Texan for nearly) turned that poor woman inside out. When they finally got to the baby, it was all they could do to pull him out. I don't know why he held on like he did. If he had been seeing what I was seeing, he'd have wanted out of there fast.

Anyway, all of us need to be educated on the finer points of C-sections and face-lifts. And if you're gonna read a book by someone, you probably want to know that person is well versed in many areas of life. We don't need no more dumb authors![1]

Hopefully, by now you know there is a method to my madness, and somehow—perhaps minutely, but somehow—this relates to our subject. The New Testament speaks of our minds having a "veil" (*kalupsis*), which prohibits us from understanding spiritual matters:

> Even if our gospel is veiled, it is veiled to those who are perishing, in whose case the god of this world has blinded the minds of the unbelieving, that they might not see the light of the gospel of the glory of Christ, who is the image of God.
>
> 2 Corinthians 4:3–4

Kalupsis simply means "to hide or cover." My lexicons said the inside of a tree is veiled by bark; the inside of a human body is veiled by skin. I understood immediately!

Interestingly, a "revelation" comes from the same Greek word; it is *kalupsis* with the prefix *apo* added—

apokalupsis. Apo means "off" or "away," so literally a revelation is an unveiling or uncovering. As I watched those surgeries, I received a revelation of the inside of a human body—at least some of it.

God wants to reveal "inside" information to us. This "intel" could be special insight into a verse of Scripture, the solution to a problem we've been asking Him about, or some direction we've been seeking. Any information revealed to us by the Holy Spirit, versus information we glean intellectually, is *revelation.*

> Yet we do speak wisdom among those who are mature; a wisdom, however, not of this age, nor of the rulers of this age, who are passing away; but we speak God's wisdom in a mystery, the hidden wisdom, which God predestined before the ages to our glory; the wisdom which none of the rulers of this age has understood; for if they had understood it, they would not have crucified the Lord of glory; but just as it is written, "Things which eye has not seen and ear has not heard, and which have not entered the heart of man, all that God has prepared for those who love Him." For to us God revealed them through the Spirit; for the Spirit searches all things, even the depths of God.
>
> 1 Corinthians 2:6–10

It should come as no surprise that the primary place to receive revelation is the Lord's presence. He wants to speak to us, not shout from far away. Spending time with God and His Word allows Him access to our minds.

175

Like a surgeon with a scalpel He can peel back the veil, revealing to us spiritual insights and His wisdom for our lives. Paul spoke of this wisdom and revelation to the Corinthians.

When we're with Him, we're in the presence of omniscience. The psalmist said God's understanding is "infinite"; Isaiah called it "inscrutable" (see Psalm 147:5; Isaiah 40:28). What an offer. We have an open invitation into the presence of One with immeasurable knowledge, infinite wisdom, and limitless understanding.

The power of the revelation flowing in Christ's presence can be seen through a meeting He had with some of His early followers. As He was beginning His earthly ministry, Jesus visited John the Baptist, who publically announced concerning Him, "Behold, the Lamb of God who takes away the sin of the world!" (John 1:29, 36). Two of John's disciples heard this stunning announcement and decided to check.

As they followed Him, Jesus noticed, turned to them, and asked, "What do you seek?"

Their answer was interesting. "Rabbi (which translated means 'Teacher'), where are you staying?"

"Come, and you will see," was His invitation to them. They took Him up on His offer and ended up spending the day with Him (v. 39).

If you're happy with things as they are, spending a day with Jesus isn't a good idea! Having a private audience with Him for an entire day is going to change you. Radically. The conversation might be superficial at first:

"How did you make trees? How many stars are there? How about galaxies?" From there, perhaps you would segue into questions concerning Jesus and God: "How old were you when you first realized who you were? What does God look like?" At some point, however, you would no doubt transition into personal questions concerning you and your future. Everyone thinks about purpose. Experts tell us the desire to know our purpose is one of the strongest desires we humans have. Believing we have a purpose is directly related to self-esteem, self-worth, and, ultimately, personal fulfillment.

Did these two men ask Jesus about this? We don't know for certain. We do know that one of them was Andrew, Simon Peter's brother (v. 40), who became one of Christ's twelve disciples. Something he heard while with Jesus impacted him so greatly he decided on a career change! Destiny flows from days spent with Jesus.

Another revelation Andrew received that day had to do not with his own identity but Christ's. He began the day by referring to Jesus as a teacher ("Rabbi"); he ended it by calling Him the Messiah. "He found first his own brother Simon, and said to him, 'We have found the Messiah' (which translated means Christ)" (John 1:41).

Andrew received the two most important revelations needed for a successful life that day: who *Christ* is, which is the key to unlocking everything else in life, and who *he* was. When those two things are known, they unlock destiny. The purpose of anything is found in the mind of its creator, not in itself. Self-identity comes from identifying and knowing the One who made us. You'll never really find yourself until you find Him. Andrew found both that day.

At the end of Christ's ministry, two more of His followers had a revelatory encounter with Him. The meeting occurred just after the cross; to say their world had turned topsy-turvy would be a gross understatement. To have discovered, lived with, and traveled with Jesus for three years, only to lose Him, would be life's cruelest injustice.

These two men had heard earlier in the day that Christ had risen from the dead. But, really, who would believe two grief-stricken ladies claiming to have been visited by angels? That's quite a stretch. And these supposed angels informed the women that Christ rose from the dead? As they walked the seven-mile journey to Emmaus, they were discussing this too-good-to-be-true report and all that had transpired over the past few days. To say that they were discouraged, confused, and disillusioned would be an understatement.

That's when He arrived. "And it came about that while they were conversing and discussing, Jesus Himself approached, and began traveling with them. But their eyes were prevented from recognizing Him" (Luke 24:15–16).

"What are you discussing?" He wanted to know.

They gave Jesus a brief summary, expressing their surprise that He would even have to ask. "What else would we be discussing?" was their inference. It seems everyone in Jerusalem could think of little else than what had transpired with Christ the last few days, since so many of them had thought He might be the long-awaited Messiah. They spoke to Him of their devastation and also of the rumor that He had risen from the dead.

Jesus, His identity still hidden from them, "explained to them the things concerning Himself in all the Scriptures" (v. 27), including the fact that He needed to suffer and die.

Wouldn't you like to hear that recording!

Though they still didn't know it was Jesus, His words began impacting their hearts. "Were not our hearts burning within us while He was speaking to us . . . explaining the Scriptures to us?" they stated (v. 32).

When they reached their destination, the men pleaded with Jesus to spend the night. The Lord agreed to do so, and during dinner, "He took the bread and blessed it, and breaking it, He began giving it to them. And their eyes were opened and they recognized Him" (vv. 30–31). He disappeared from their sight at that moment, and they hurried back the seven miles to Jerusalem with the good news: Christ was, indeed, risen.

I find it more than a coincidence that after hiding from these men who He was, the Lord chose to release the revelation "in the breaking of the bread" (v. 35). After all, He was the "bread of life" that had been "broken" for them (see John 6:33, 35, 48–51), and they could now partake of this resurrection life. Was the timing His way of saying to them, "The sustenance you need is now available. Sup with me and I will reveal to you the things you need to know"? I believe so. I also believe it says the same to us. We can eat the bread of life. We do so by eating His words (Matthew 4:4). Eat them. As you do, revelation will come. He will unveil Himself to you, just as he did these two men. And as it was with Andrew, He will also reveal to you your purpose and destiny.

Spend a day with Jesus.

Prayer

Father, it's Your glory to conceal a thing, and it's our privilege as Your children to search those things out. Yes, thick darkness surrounds You, but You invite us into Your cloud of glory . . . to linger, to listen, to receive as You unveil, uncover, and release revelation. Thank You so much, Jesus, for making a way.

As I sit in Your presence, Lord, awaken all of my senses to receive the greatest measure of revelation I can acquire at that moment concerning Your works and Your ways. Until the next time . . . and then let's do it all over again.

I know that until we meet face-to-face, Jesus, I will still have a dimmed view of Your infinite wisdom and glory, Your power and sovereignty. Oh, how I long for that day! Until then I'll press in further and further. I want to know You in this life in every possible way.

I'd like to spend this day visiting with You, Holy Spirit, with the Scriptures laid open before me, as You search and reveal to me the mysteries, secrets, and depths of God; I want a much greater glimpse. And from there may purpose and destiny flow.

(Prayer taken from: Proverbs 25:2; Isaiah 45:3; Psalm 97:2; 2 Corinthians 4:3–4; 1 Corinthians 13:12; 1 Corinthians 2:6–10; Psalm 147:5; Isaiah 40:28; Luke 24:32; Matthew 4:4)

22

THE PRODIGAL

In the book *What Will It Take to Change the World* by S. D. Gordon, he relates the story of a couple who discovered that their fourteen-year-old son— we'll call him Steven—had lied to them. He had skipped school for three consecutive days and was caught when his concerned teacher called his parents to inquire about his well-being.

The parents were obviously very concerned, more so over his lies than over his missing school. After thinking about and discussing the situation, they decided on a very unusual and severe form of punishment. For the next three days, one for each day of his sin, he would be grounded to the attic, even eating and sleeping there. Steven had no choice but to accept the punishment, and headed off to the attic.

It was a long evening for Mom and Dad, perhaps even more so than for Steven. At dinner neither could eat, and after a seemingly interminable evening, at last it was bedtime. But bedtime brought no relief. As the hours ticked by, both lay awake thinking about how lonely and afraid Steven must be. At 2:00 a.m. Dad could stand it no longer. "I'm going to the attic," he muttered as he grabbed a blanket and pillow. He was not surprised to find Steven still awake and in tears.

"Steven," said his father, "I can't take away the punishment for your lies because you must know the seriousness of what you have done. You realize that sin, especially lying, has severe consequences. But your mother and I can't bear the thought of you being all alone here in the attic, so I'm going to share your punishment with you."

Then he lay down alongside his son and the two put their arms around each other. The father's tears mingled with the son's as they shared the same pillow and the same punishment.

What a picture! Two thousand years ago God crawled "out of bed" with His blanket and pillow—actually three spikes and a cross of crucifixion—"staked" His tearstained cheek next to ours, and bore our punishment for sin. His attic was a tomb, His bed a slab of rock, and the cheek next to His was yours—yours and mine.[1]

Our sin doesn't lessen God's love for us.

I mentioned previously that I ran from God for a couple of years. Actually, I wasn't running from Him;

I was running from my pain. When I was seventeen, my father, who was a pastor, fell into adultery and subsequently left our family. It was devastating. (He repented a few years later, was restored to the Lord, and is now in heaven. We had a wonderful relationship the last thirty years of his life.) In my pain and confusion I turned to drugs and alcohol. The Lord was gracious and patient, and pursued me for two years. I ran hard, but He persevered and loved me back to Him.

For those two years of wandering I had a very skewed impression of my heavenly Father. While I was thinking of Him as angry, He was actually feeling my pain. Scripture tells us that Jesus, our High Priest representing us in heaven, sympathizes with our weaknesses, having been tempted with all the temptations we face (Hebrews 4:15). He also experienced rejection, betrayal, and the pain of broken relationships. The Lord knows how to comfort us.

Father God wasn't condoning my sin, but He was merciful and patient. His desire was to heal and cleanse me, not dole out condemnation and punishment. Ultimately, as the old hymn so clearly states, "when nothing else could help, love lifted me."[2]

Most Christians know the story of the prodigal son, told by Jesus in Luke 15. This young man took his inheritance while his father was still alive, left home, and "squandered his estate with loose living" (Luke 15:13). Actually, the term *prodigal* doesn't mean "lost," "away from," or "runaway" as many think; it means "recklessly wasteful; extravagant consumer; a squanderer." He was "the squandering son."

Just as in our opening story, one of the primary points of the prodigal's story is the heart of the father. Both are great pictures of our heavenly Father, who is quick to forgive and is even willing to restore our squandered inheritance. When the son returned home,

> While he was still a long way off, his father saw him and felt compassion for him, and ran and embraced him and kissed him. . . . The father said to his slaves, "Quickly bring out the best robe and put it on him, and put a ring on his hand and sandals on his feet."
>
> vv. 20, 22

If you—like the prodigal, the boy in the attic, or me—have sinned against God, His desire is to restore you. I pray that you find repentance and return to Him. Before you make any effort to repent, however, let's make sure you understand what repentance is. We've misunderstood this word, just as we have *prodigal*. Biblically, *repentance* doesn't mean "turn from sin"; nor does it mean "remorse." To be sorry for our sins is good, and to ultimately turn from them is necessary. But before these things can occur, we must receive a *change of mind*, which is the literal meaning of *metanoia*, the biblical word for repentance. "A new understanding," "think differently," and "a new knowledge" would all be good definitions of repentance.

The prodigal found repentance. The passage tells us,

"He came to his senses" (Luke 15:17). In the midst of his pain, shame, lack, and condemnation, the young man finally woke up. *I could live better than this as one of my father's servants*, he thought to himself. With a new outlook, he returned home, humbled himself, and confessed his sins.

The repentance I experienced was that God wasn't angry at me. He wasn't disappointed with me, nor was He condemning and threatening me with hell's fire. To the contrary, He came to me in a bar one night, put His cheek next to mine, and shared the pain of my sin. He also helped me grieve the loss of my father. I received a revelation of His love and of my condition (repentance), told God I was sorry, and turned from my sin.

The Lord restored me to Himself—and to my inheritance. If you have failed in some way, or perhaps even run from God, He will do the same for you. Don't accept a lie that says your sin lessens His love for you. God runs to meet His returning kids. He needs your humility, sometimes even your brokenness, but never the crippling paralysis caused by condemnation.

Toward the end of the 19th century, Swedish chemist Alfred Nobel awoke one morning to read his own obituary in the local newspaper: "Alfred Nobel, the inventor of dynamite, who died yesterday, devised a way for more people to be killed in a war than ever before, and he died a very rich man."

Actually, it was Alfred's older brother who had died; a reporter had botched the obituary. The account had a profound effect on Alfred Nobel. He decided that he wanted to be known for something other than inventing the means for killing people in war, and for amassing great wealth in the process.

So he initiated the Nobel Peace Prize, the award for those who foster peace. He said, "Every man ought to have the chance to correct his epitaph in midstream and write a new one."[3]

Your story isn't over—go home to Dad.

Prayer

Father, I thank You for entrusting me with so much and sharing all that You have. I don't want to be a prodigal and squander my inheritance. I want to be a good son and a good steward of Your promises and provision. Holy Sprit, help me to ascribe worth and rightly handle every spiritual blessing extended to me through the gift of Your Son.

Truly You are good in every way, God—a faithful Friend, loving Father, and gracious Comforter. You've never given up on me. My eyes are freshly opened; I can see more clearly now. I repent and turn from the waywardness within me.

Thank You for drawing me home to Your heart with cords of kindness. Thank You for restoring me. Father, I love Your house! This is where I belong; the place where Your goodness and glory dwell. All my fears and failures fall away when I'm in Your sweet company. It's here that I long to remain.

(Prayer taken from: Luke 15:11–32; Deuteronomy 18:1–2; Matthew 6:19–20; Ephesians 1:3; Hebrews 2:18; Hebrews 4:15; John 14:16; Joel 2:13; Lamentations 3:40; Psalm 26:8; John 14:2)

THE RETURN

I like older things. I'm sure it has nothing to do with the fact that I'm fifty-eight-years OLD! (Ceci wanted to make sure you know I married a *much* younger woman.) I like antiquing, watching TV shows like *American Pickers* and *American Restoration*, shopping in old stores, and studying history. Ceci and I have always liked vacationing in places that cater more to older folks. I'm not sure how I got old so fast. Now that I'm pushing sixty I'm trying to renegotiate.

While I do like older things, I don't like fixing or restoring them. I've never been into restoring furniture, homes, or cars. I tried to restore an engine once—never did figure out where all the leftover parts went, and I couldn't understand why the stupid thing wouldn't run when I was finished. Probably a lemon.

Oh, and there was the table I once restored. Ceci was so impressed she gave it away. First she reminded me of the passage in Scripture where three of David's mighty men heard he was craving water from the well of Bethlehem. This was his hometown and the craving was probably a longing for the comforts of home. Even though the well was currently controlled by enemies, these three brave and loyal men broke through the enemy lines and brought David water from the well. He was so moved by their sacrificial love he wouldn't drink it: "Be it far from me before my God that I should [drink] this. Shall I drink the blood of those men who went at the risk of their lives?" (1 Chronicles 11:19). David poured it out as an offering to the Lord! The story has always moved me.

Knowing how much I loved it, Ceci reminded me of the noble act and compared the restored table to the water. "It's just too precious to keep," she said. "All that hard work you put into it. I think I'm going to donate it to Goodwill so a poor family that could never afford such an amazing table can enjoy it."

It moved me to tears. Still chokes me up just thinking about how much it meant to her. Anyway, that was my only successful restoration. I figured I'd better stop there or Ceci would be wanting me to do furniture restoration all the time.

Of course, some people really are into restoration and are actually good at it. God is—and He's the best. He can take hearts and lives that seem beyond repair and make them as good as new. In fact, healing broken hearts and restoring lives are both part of Christ's mission statement:

> The Spirit of the Lord is upon me, because he hath anointed me to preach the gospel to the poor; he hath sent me to heal the brokenhearted, to preach deliverance to the captives, and recovering of sight to the blind, to set at liberty them that are bruised.
>
> Luke 4:18 KJV

The Son of God finds great pleasure in healing broken hearts and bringing deliverance to those bound by sin or oppression. He's a restorer and redeemer by nature, not the mean-spirited judge many believe him to be. In his famous Twenty-third Psalm, David said of Him, "He restores my soul" (v. 3); elsewhere he said the Lord's words are powerful enough to restore our souls (Psalm 19:7).

Several years ago I counseled a young woman who had been horribly abused sexually. Her soul was broken, fractured by the pain of being abused by a family member. It was gut wrenching to listen to her speak of it, in between the sobs and wailing. Over the years she looked to drugs and alcohol, sexual promiscuity, and even cutting to find a way of escape from her painful past. Of course, none of these things helped. After several weeks I was finally able to persuade her to forgive her abuser, lower the protective walls around her heart, and allow the Lord entrance.

193

The transformation was dramatic. The pain began to lessen and was gradually replaced by peace. She began to see herself as pure—not defiled—and special to the Lord. Experiencing His love allowed her to regain self-respect. It's special to be loved by Jesus. Ultimately, her ability to trust was restored and she is now healthy in every way and enjoys the pleasure of His company. Jesus heals and restores.

He also forgives.

Christ's mission statement of love, healing, and forgiveness in Luke was actually a quote from Isaiah 61:1. A lot of Christians don't like to read the Old Testament prophets, especially those who speak of judgment. But these prophets get a bad rap, and so does God. Their writings, though including predictions of judgment, actually have more to do with forgiveness. Most judgment is not the direct hand of God, but the automatic reaping built into sinful actions, an inevitable reaping of what we have sown. Disobedience, sin, and idolatry pay painful wages (Romans 6:23). God built in sin's painful payday in order to deter us from what He knew would harm us, not because He is cruel.

When we do sin, His message to us, just as it was to Israel through the prophets, is "return to me" and be forgiven (see Isaiah 44:22; 55:7; Zachariah 1:3; Malachi 3:7). The New Testament tells us, "If we confess our sins, He is faithful and righteous to forgive us our sins and to cleanse us from all unrighteousness" (1 John 1:9). When the returning takes place, the restoration begins. Both terms are actually the same Hebrew word in Scripture (*shuwb*). When we *return* to God, we're *restored* to wholeness and purpose.

In John's gospel he shares the account of a woman caught in the act of adultery. The Pharisees brought the woman to Jesus, asking His opinion as to what should be done with her.

> The scribes and Pharisees brought a woman caught in adultery, and having set her in the midst, they said to Him, Teacher, this woman has been caught in adultery, in the very act. Now the Law Moses commanded us to stone such women; what then do You say?"
>
> John 8:3–5

Jesus didn't answer them but stooped and began writing in the dirt. No one knows what He wrote, but they persisted in their asking. The response He finally gave is now famous: "He who is without sin among you, let him be the first to throw a stone at her" (v. 7). Then He stooped to write once more. Again, we don't know what He wrote—some surmise He was writing some of their hidden sins—but while He wrote they began to leave.

Jesus stood and asked her, "Woman, where are they? Did no one condemn you?"

She said, "No one, Lord."

Then came another of Christ's famous sayings: "I do not condemn you either. Go. From now on sin no more" (v. 11).

What a wonderful story of forgiveness. Christ is

looking to restore us, not condemn us. His forgiveness of this woman does nothing to lessen the wrongness of adultery. What it does do is exemplify the level and overwhelming power of Christ's redeeming love. He is waiting to redeem, not condemn.

Our distorted perception of God's intentions is well illustrated by the urban legend of a woman driving home alone one evening when she noticed a man in a large truck following her. Growing increasingly fearful, she sped up, trying to lose her pursuer, but it was futile. She then exited the freeway and drove up a main street, but the truck stayed with her, even running red lights to do so.

In a panic, the woman wheeled into a service station, jumped from the car, and ran inside screaming. The truck driver ran to her car, jerked the back door open, and pulled from the floor behind her seat a man hiding there.

The woman was fleeing from the wrong person. *She was running from her savior!* The truck driver, perched high enough to see into her back seat, had spied the would-be rapist and was pursuing her to save her, even at his own peril.

So often we run from God, fearing His wrath while He is pursuing us to save us from destruction. He wants only our best, and died to provide it. Instead of seeing Him as our Savior, however, we sometimes see only the promise of loss and a lack of fulfillment. I urge you—if you have sinned, stop running from the wrong person. Return to God and allow Him to forgive you and heal you.

In the popular comic strip *Calvin and Hobbes*, by Bill Watterson, Calvin tells his tiger friend, Hobbes, that he feels bad for calling his schoolmate Susie names. When Hobbes suggests Calvin apologize, Calvin ponders for a moment and replies, "I keep hoping there's a less obvious solution."[1]

There isn't a less obvious solution. If you have unforgiven sin in your life, run to Jesus and apologize. He's not waiting with a belt but with His atoning blood. One of my favorite hymns is one I remember from my earliest days.

> There is a fountain filled with blood,
> Drawn from Emmanuel's veins;
> And sinners plunged beneath that flood
> Lose all their guilty stains.[2]

Millions have bathed under this fountain and lost their guilty stains. Your sin is no match for the cleansing power of His shed blood, nor is your pain. The cross proves His love.

Take the plunge.

Prayer

What a good and gracious Father You are; not only forgiving us when we return to You, but healing hearts and restoring lives too. Jesus, Your mandate of redemption is so noble, and You are faithful to fulfill it when we come to You, even when we seem to be beyond repair. I'm so grateful for the cleansing power of Your blood.

The truth is that You have only good intentions toward me. Still I so often run from You, God. Help me, Holy Spirit, not to focus on my frail condition but on God's saving grace and loving might that's here to lift me. I repent. I'll stop running and return to You.

Your Word is powerful enough to completely restore my soul, to strengthen me and give me wings for flight; I choose to meditate upon it now. Your good desire for me is to enjoy the pleasure of Your company, and from that place of wholeness, trust and rest, then run and soar.

(Prayer taken from: Luke 4:18; Psalm 23:3; Psalm 19:7; Isaiah 44:22; Isaiah 55:7; Zachariah 1:3; Malachi 3:7; 1 John 1:9; Titus 2:11; Hebrews 4:16; Isaiah 40:31)

24

THE REVELATION

I was pretty good at football. Actually, I was really good. Oh well, why be so humble? I was great. (You've probably heard about the guy who won an award for being the most humble; they took it away from him because he wore the badge.)

Actually, I was decent in football and a step below that in basketball and track. I worked really hard at them, especially football. Unlike some of the more gifted athletes, I had to be very diligent to attain any level of success. I did start at quarterback for three years in high school, but it was my tenacious work ethic that enabled me to do so, not natural ability.

I found much of my identity in athletics. Growing up as a very insecure kid, I needed the success of sports to feel good about myself. As I excelled, I also became popular and was able to hide my insecurities and the accompanying fears of failure and rejection. Without my realizing it was happening, my self-esteem became performance based. My self-acceptance was not based on internal well-being, but was measured entirely by how well I performed.

My success in sports, along with my popularity and the subconscious coping mechanisms I had built into my personality, kept me from realizing how insecure I really was. Our souls can look very different on the outside than they actually are inwardly. We can even fool ourselves, creating what have come to be called blind spots. We probably all have a few. Call them what you want—I was in trouble and didn't know it.

When I became a student at Christ For The Nations in 1977, through my spending time with Him, the Lord began identifying my inward condition to me. The process began due to intense jealousy I felt toward another student because of his gifts and popularity.

For several days I tried to deny those feelings. Thinking I was pushing them *away*, I was actually pushing them *down* into some hidden hole in my soul. I believed I could keep them from gaining a hold on me by denying them. But like a rubber ball in a swimming pool, the jealousy kept popping back up. What I didn't want to admit was that these feelings originated from within me, not as a temptation from without. My deep and camouflaged insecurities were reacting to someone else's success, and I had no Friday night game through which to offset the feelings.

The Holy Spirit began speaking to me about this, challenging me to acknowledge that the jealousy actually existed *within* me, not as a temptation. I argued with these "thoughts," refusing to believe they were the voice of the Holy Spirit. He persisted, however, and eventually prevailed. I could no longer deny it, but I didn't know how to evict it.

To most people, the fact that they experienced some jealousy may not have been as big a deal as it was to me. A secure individual would probably have acknowledged it, asked God to help them deal with it, and moved on. I, however, was an insecure perfectionist; I "performed" for His acceptance, as well as for others'. I felt condemnation for having this problem and anger that I couldn't overcome it. I remember finally blurting out to God, "Okay, I'm jealous! I have issues."

He probably smiled.

"I'm not upset or disappointed with you that this weakness exists," I heard Him say clearly. "I know how it got there and that you had no control over the process. I just want to get rid of it."

I knew this was the Holy Spirit speaking to me and was shocked that He wasn't angry or disappointed with me. From that moment my perception of God began to change. Looking back, I see now my whole world began to change. Yahweh started becoming my Father, not just my God.

In the ensuing days, once I began to trust His heart, He started focusing on the cause, not just the effect. Jealousy was a symptom; deep insecurities were the root. Again, initially I resisted somewhat. *I'm not insecure,* I thought. *I'm outgoing, popular, friendly. I'm very secure.*

But again, the Holy Spirit lovingly persisted, giving me some evidence. "You manipulate relationships to be in control. You're talkative and outgoing, but that is not really the personality I gave you. It is actually something you developed in order to be thought of as cool and funny. When you are engaged in a conversation, you aren't really listening to the other person; you're thinking about what to say next in order to sound interesting, intelligent, or funny. You're always posturing and performing for acceptance . . . even with Me. If you don't allow Me to heal this in you, one day it will cost you your destiny."

I was stunned. Over the next couple of weeks I began to clearly see these things about myself. If I was speaking with someone, the Holy Spirit would point out the behavior. "There, you just did what I described to you." When these manifestations occurred and He pointed them out, I was eventually able to see the patterns and acknowledge my performance issues.

Finally, I said to the Lord, "Okay, I see the fears and insecurities in me. What do I do?" Through my quiet times He guided me to verses of Scripture on which to meditate; He spoke to my heart in ways that brought comfort, healing, reassurance, and strength. His Father-heart was amazing.

As He healed me, my personality actually changed. The real me is quiet and somewhat introverted by nature. I enjoy being alone. God made me this way. It is necessary that I enjoy solitude in order to study, think, pray, write, and spend much of life alone in hotel rooms. Also, I no longer feel a need to "perform" for acceptance. I have nothing to prove and am secure in being who He created me to be.

When God reveals weaknesses in our lives, it is not to condemn us. His goal is closure, not exposure. His fire is to refine us, and His faceting machine, like that of a master jeweler, is to shape us into the finest diamond possible. He knows how and where we can shine the most. God is our Father, not a taskmaster; a Shepherd, not a hireling. Trust His heart and ways. Our wise Creator makes no mistakes, never miscalculates, and has no bad performance days. His ways are perfect.

The psalmist David learned to trust God. "Search me," he said, "and know my heart; try me and know my anxious thoughts; And see if there be any hurtful way in me, And lead me in the everlasting way" (Psalm 139:23–24). "Hurtful" is from the Hebrew word *otseb*, meaning "pain, whether mental or bodily, sorrow, or a harmful habit," including idolatry and other forms of wickedness. David was saying, "I don't know myself as well as I think I do, Lord. Perhaps you'd better take a look inside and check things out. See if my heart has any blockages or valve problems; analyze my soul and show me my blind spots. Look into my emotions and reveal any buried pain or unhealed wounds. Perhaps I've lived with them so long I've learned to compensate, mistaking coping mechanisms for true health. I believe that you will lead me out of any problems you find, and into your wonderful ways of healing."

Maybe we should pray a prayer such as this.

The Great Physician knows us better than we know ourselves. Trust Him with your heart. You'll never fully know the pleasure of His company until you experience it with a healthy heart. Don't "perform" for your Father's love and acceptance, settling for a superficial relationship. You were made for more, much more.

Today begins the new.

Prayer

Your love, Father, is amazing! You refuse to let us live with the secret pain of hidden, unhealed wounds. You take time to gently highlight the issues of my heart while inviting me to crawl up into Your lap, lay my head upon Your chest, and then let Your gentle hands get to work.

Healing and wholeness are the outcome of Your work in me; loving-kindness and compassion are Your tools. There's never a lecture condemning my faults, just a much-needed revelation of my need. And if I fully yield, You'll remove not just the symptoms of my weakness, You'll be sure to get right to the root.

Today I lay my pride aside so I can I lift up a prayer like David's. Lord, search my heart; examine all my thoughts and ways. Show me the patterns that point to my condition—the manifestations of the illness in my heart.

Great Physician, I place myself upon Your table, surrendering my all. Set Your healing hands upon me now—a painstaking process, yet worth it all. Guide me, Holy Spirit, in applying the medicine of Scripture to every area of my life. I want to fully experience the healing balm that is the pleasure of Your company.

(Prayer taken from: Psalm 103:1–14; Psalm 51:1–13; Psalm 26:2–3; Psalm 139:23–24; Psalm 107:19–22; Lamentations 3:40; Ephesians 5:26–27; Acts 22:16; Isaiah 53:4)

25

THE LOOK

One of the things I like about the Bible is that God allows its heroes of faith to be real, choosing not to hide their humanness from the rest of us all-too-human earthlings. Pedestals are great for nonhuman displays, but they're far too unstable to support the average human. There are worries concerning this when it comes to the Scriptures. The Bible puts the average reality TV show to shame. Affairs, murders, betrayals, failures—all the zits are there.

Simon Peter is one of those real-life characters. I love his realness. A down-to-earth fisherman, grinding out a living in the small town of Capernaum on the Sea of Galilee, Peter was probably a tough, calloused, hard-nosed individual. This outspoken disciple sometimes wore his emotions on his sleeve—he once rebuked Jesus

(Matthew 16:22) and later cut off the ear of the high priest's servant at the Lord's arrest (John 18:10)—and, like many good fishermen, was known to string out a few expletives when necessary (Matthew 26:24).

Like any good carpenter with a raw piece of wood, Jesus could see past the knots and blemishes in Peter to the potential within. *I like this guy,* He must have thought. *A little rough around the edges, but great potential.* He may have even mused, somewhat pensively as His prophetic gift kicked in, *He is so loyal, in fact, that one day he'll be willing to die for me* (see John 13:36; 21:18). "Follow me!" He shouted to Peter and his brother Andrew one fateful day. The rest, as they say, is history.

One of Peter's all-too-human moments came at the Last Supper, the night before Christ's crucifixion. Like many of us, he was a bit overconfident concerning his commitment to the Master. When Jesus spoke of His arrest and of the disciples' scattering, Peter spoke up and bragged, "I'll never run. I'm ready to go to prison and die for you" (Luke 22:33, paraphrased).

I'm sure Peter believed his level of commitment was this great. Christ, however, knew better and gave Peter the now famous "before the cock crows, you'll deny me three times" prophecy (v. 34). Evidently the Lord wasn't the only one seeing the potential in Peter. Satan wanted him out of the picture. "Simon, Simon," Jesus told Peter.

> Behold, Satan has demanded permission to sift you like wheat; but I have prayed for you, that your faith may

not fail; and you, when once you have turned again, strengthen your brothers.

vv. 31–32

Rather than being offended or "put out" with Peter due to his impending betrayal, He was compassionate toward him. "I have prayed for you," the Lord said, "and because of that you'll make it through this ordeal."

The Lord knows that in the course of life all of us will fail Him. If He demanded perfection, where would any of us be? Jesus was aware of Peter's weaknesses, but He also knew that deep in him was a faithful heart, and He was determined to mine the gold. He is committed to your development and success, as well. He won't give up on you.

The Lord's prediction concerning Peter came true later that night. He did, indeed, deny Christ three times. I've always believed Peter's denial was born more of confusion than fear. Confusion disorients and leads to fear, which in turn produces loss of courage and paralysis. Peter was experiencing all of the above. Initially, he was ready to fight for Jesus; a few hours earlier when the Lord was arrested, he had drawn a sword and cut off the ear of the high priest's slave. But Jesus had chosen not to resist arrest, and now things were spiraling out of control.

Having followed Christ to His trial, he was watching the proceedings from a distance when three times he was accused of being one of His disciples. By the time the third accusation came, things were in chaos—Christ was being slapped around, beaten, and spat upon, and a dangerous mob-like atmosphere was forming.

In what must have been a confused state of panic, Peter buckled under the pressure. "I don't know Him!" he shouted, peppering his denial with bad language. Scripture says, "He began to curse and swear" (Matthew 26:74). Obviously, it was more than one expletive.

I find what happened next very moving. Jesus was close enough to hear him, and upon doing so, "turned and looked at Peter" (Luke 22:61). We're left to guess what kind of look He gave Peter, but it certainly wasn't one of shock or surprise; after all, He predicted the denial. Another possibility would be that the Lord gave him an angry, condemning, I-can't-believe-you-just-did-that look. Knowing Christ as I do, I can't believe this was the look He gave Peter, either.

Though obviously it cannot be proven, I'm reasonably confident the look Jesus gave this troubled and confused fisherman—who had left everything to follow Him—was one of deep compassion and reassurance: "Don't worry, Peter, I understand. And I still believe in you. Remember, I saw this coming and prayed for you. Everything is going to be all right."

If I'm correct, to think that Christ had the presence of mind at this point to be concerned about someone else's well-being is amazing. One would think His response, if not surprise or anger, would have at least been something like, "I'm a little busy right now redeeming the world, Peter, and things are getting a little intense. Sorry, but you're on your own." But Jesus was no ordinary man. Even while on the cross, one moment He was comforting a thief, the next making sure His mother was going to be taken care of. In keeping with his character and the nature of His earlier comments, I believe he gave Peter a loving and reassuring look. I also believe that with one glance He saved Peter's destiny.

Seeing Christ's look, Peter was undone. One can only imagine the flood of emotion he was experiencing. In Gethsemane, he had just seen Christ literally bleed through the pores of His skin, a condition called hematidrosis. Then came the arrest and beatings—Christ's face and clothing must have been covered in blood and spittle. And now this. Overcome with emotion, Peter fled the trial and "wept bitterly" (Luke 22:62).

The emotional roller coaster continued with the cross, three days of mourning, followed by the resurrection. As thrilled as the disciples were to see Jesus alive, however, things were still not the same. He kept vanishing and reappearing, only to leave again. He was gone most of the time. Finally, Peter had had enough. All of this was way above his pay grade. We're not sure of his exact train of thought, but I'm guessing it was similar to this: *I'm no rabbi or theologian; and I'm not a prophet, with the ability to understand mysteries and see into the future. I don't understand all of this theology, and certainly not the events of the last few days. Nothing has worked out the way I expected; I have no idea where Jesus is. I'm going back to the only thing I really understand right now.* "I am going fishing," he said to several of the other disciples (John 21:3).

Also confused and unable to connect the dots, they simply said, "We're going with you."

I suppose it's possible these guys were just needing some rest and rehabilitation, but I don't think so. I believe they were finished. Having gone home to Capernaum on the Sea of Galilee, it doesn't take much imagination to think they were likely sitting around asking one another, "What do we do now? How do we make a living, pay the bills?" Finally, one of them stated the obvious, "Well, we still have the boat."

"Yep," answered Peter, "and I'm goin' fishin'."

I imagine the Lord was sympathetic to their plight. He caused it, after all, and He loved them. He knew if they could just hang on until Pentecost they would make it. So He told Dad, Holy Spirit, and Gabriel He was going to make another earthly appearance. "The guys could use another encouraging word, especially Peter. I'm going to go cook them breakfast, visit with them awhile, and help them pay some bills."

And that's exactly what He did.

After they had finished a fruitless night of fishing, Jesus was waiting on the beach at daybreak. When they were about a hundred yards from shore, He shouted, "Did you catch any fish?" The Lord knew they hadn't caught any; He probably caused their fruitless night so He could get their attention with what He was about to do!

"No," they responded, still unable to recognize Him.

"Cast the net on the right-hand side of the boat, and you will find a catch" (John 21:6).

Bells must have started ringing, reminding them of an earlier encounter with Him, when He helped them reap a great catch and subsequently invited them to follow Him (Luke 5:1–11). With the similarities, they must have wondered, but . . . *No way. It couldn't be Him.*

They decided to give His plan a try and, sure enough, caught more fish than they could drag into the boat. John, now certain, said, "It is the Lord" (v. 7). And Peter—you just have to love this guy—was so excited he decided to jump in and swim ashore. Why not wait until the boat could be rowed the hundred yards to shore? Not Peter! Surely you can see his great love for Jesus. He was so flustered that rather than take some of his clothing *off* to make the swim easier, he put his coat *on* and dove into the water. Impetuous? Perhaps. But also passionate.

Jesus must have smiled. He already had a fire going and food cooking. "Come and have breakfast," He invited them. It must have brought back great memories to all of them. We don't know everything they talked about, but the pleasure of His company must have been wonderfully reassuring.

Eventually, knowing Peter was probably still grieving over his earlier denial of Him, Jesus began addressing the situation. Three times He asked Peter if he loved Him, and each time Peter responded affirmatively. Some theologians believe Jesus asked the question three times in order to offset Peter's three denials. Perhaps, but the first time He asked Peter the question, Jesus added the question, "Do you love Me *more than these*?" (v. 15, italics mine). Was He referring to the other disciples, or was He referencing the fish? I believe Jesus was referring to the fish, which represented Peter's former livelihood and career. Could this be why He chose to meet them at the same location where their original calling had occurred, and why He worked the exact same miracle? If that wasn't enough, He then gave Peter the same command—twice—as He had on that first occasion. "Follow Me!" He said to him (v. 19).

When Peter tried to deflect the attention from himself to John, Jesus would have none of it. "If I want him to remain until I come, what is that to you? You follow me!" (v. 22). Notice the exclamation points. These are, indeed, commands in the Greek tense they were written in. Jesus was saying to this uncertain fisherman: "Your calling hasn't changed, Peter. I still need you, and it will be to catch men, not fish. Your failure didn't disqualify you; and the fact that I'm not around at the present time hasn't changed the plan. Hang in there—everything will make sense in a few more days."

And it did.

On the day of Pentecost, Peter was born again and filled with the Holy Spirit. The Christ who used to walk beside Him now lived in Him. Peter preached that day, and three thousand people were born again! A few days later he healed a lame man known by the entire city of Jerusalem, and five thousand more people were saved!

He had made it.

The crusty, foul-mouthed, impetuous, confused denier had survived his trauma and made it through the most confusing and consequential season in world history. He came into the new era of redeemed humankind with strength and purpose. You'll make it, too. If and when you fail Him—and most of us will—look for the look. It'll be there. Understand the temporariness of setbacks. When you're grieving and confused, He wants to take you to breakfast, not expel you from the family.

Follow Him!

Prayer

Father, I am so grateful that You look past the external deficiencies and search deep within, mining for the gold that's within my heart. Jesus, You were fully aware of Peter's weaknesses yet focused on the faithfulness that through humble love and compassion You were able to see in Him.

Thank You, Lord, for Your commitment to my development and success. I stand amazed—You've never given up on me! Even when I'm full of confusion, fear, and failure-induced shame, You lovingly whisper to me, "Look up, my child," and with one glance of Your eyes, I'm undone. Comfort, confidence, and new strength arise within me.

Today I choose to sit face-to-face and stare back into Your intense gaze. Identity, destiny, and everything I need I'll find in those fiery eyes that are burning with passion for me. I will follow You, Jesus, and look for the look that is everything.

(Prayer taken from: 1 Samuel 16:7; Revelation 1:14; Psalm 25:15; 2 Chronicles 6:19; Psalm 145:15; Leviticus 26:9; Luke 22:61–62)

26

THE ALTAR

Have you ever been lost? I have. Well, not *really* lost. I'm a man, you understand. We don't get lost; we simply drive around for hours because we like to take the scenic route. It's entertainment. After a few hours we stop to "use the restroom" and very discreetly check with someone else to confirm that we're not *really* lost.

"Yep, right on target," we declare to our passengers. "All we do is . . ." The most I've not *really* been lost is ninety miles.

I recall the time I wasn't *really* lost in the woods. I was hunting in an area of Colorado that was new to me. We arrived at our cabin late in the afternoon and I decided to take advantage of the last couple hours of daylight. *I'll just go scout around a little,* I thought.

This will give me a slight advantage in the morning. And who knows, I might even get lucky and see an elk. Better take my gun.

I scouted around twenty minutes too long. This meant a lengthy walk back to the cabin in the dark. No problem. I had my flashlight, compass, and survival gear. I wasn't scared. That's why I whistled and hummed as I walked. I always whistle and hum in a woods at night when I'm not *really* lost and not *really* scared.

Somewhere I missed a turn. Things look different going the opposite direction, especially in the dark.

Nothing jump-starts the imagination like being alone and lost—well, not *really* lost—in an unknown woods at night. (Not that I was scared, you understand.) Creatures I don't even believe in live in unknown woods at night. I heard noises that were downright weird. I also walked past approximately ten mountain lions and five bears. Luckily, they heard me whistling, detected my confidence, and ran off. It helps to be smarter than they are.

In times like these, at some point the mind begins to think crazy thoughts and ask strange questions. *I know all elk are supposed to be vegetarians, but I wonder if some are really meat eaters?* I recall thinking. *They don't have deductive reasoning like we humans, but could they possibly know why I'm out here?*

"Naw!" I heard myself say out loud.

Then for some unknown reason I also heard myself say very loudly, "Sure is a great night for a walk. I hope no elk think I've been hunting them."

Suddenly something jumped near the trail. Limbs and branches cracked and the ground shook as something sounding like a horse rumbled through the night. I think it was a Sasquatch. After I set a new record for the 400-meter dash, I slowed down to 50 mph and congratulated myself for having the calmness to take advantage of this time alone to enjoy some jogging. If you're going to be almost but not *really* lost in the woods, you might as well get in a little aerobic exercise.

"Most guys would never think of that," I bragged to myself. "They'd be too scared." Finally I came to the main road. I was only a mile or two south of where I wanted to be. *Not bad*, I thought.

As I approached the cabin, my concerned buddies were outside waiting for me. "We were starting to get a little worried," they said. "Were you lost?"

"Not really," I replied.

"Probably just wanted a little exercise, right?" they remarked in a matter-of-fact manner. Guys understand things like this.[1]

We humans aren't really lost. We're just wandering around the planet exercising in the darkness. The reality of our denial is often lost to us. (Think about it.) Admitting our lost condition is the first step to being found. The next step? The cross.

The streets of London can be challenging to navigate. The city is huge and its streets meander in different directions. I've been there on numerous occasions, and most of the time I have no idea where I am or how I got there. I simply leave it to my hosts and the cabbies. There are certain landmarks that serve as good reference points for the locals. One of them is the Charing Cross. Near the center of the city, it is known by most Londoners.

A little girl was lost in this overwhelming maze of concrete, rivers, buildings, and roundabouts. A bobby, the informal term for a British policeman, found her wandering the streets. Between her sobs and tears she explained to the bobby that she was lost. "I don't know my way home," she cried. The policeman asked her for her address. "I don't know what it is," she said, even more panicky.

"What is your phone number?" he inquired. She didn't know that, either. "Is there anything at all you can think of?" the kind bobby asked the little girl. Suddenly, her face lit up.

"I know the cross," she exclaimed. "Take me to the cross. I can find my way home from there."[2]

The lost have been finding their way home through the cross for two thousand years. Easy to find yet missed by many, it marks the way to Father's house. I love the cross—it was there that I first found the pleasure of His company. Frequent visits there to think and meditate are recommended.

God hid pictures of the cross in the Old Testament. The pieces of furniture in the Tabernacle, for instance, were in the shape of a cross. Other pictures came not through an object's shape but its message or meaning.

One of these was a mountain named Ebal. Located across the valley from it was another mountain, Gerizim, and these two mountains became very significant.

Ebal was barren and rocky—that's where it got its name, which means "stony heap of barrenness." Gerizim, on the other hand, was fertile and lush. Consistent with their names, Ebal became the mountain associated with the curses and judgments associated with sin, Gerizim with the blessings of redemption. It was on these two mountains that the curses resulting from disobedience and the blessings associated with obedience were read to the twelve tribes of Israel (Joshua 8:30–35). These blessings and curses can be found in their entirety in Deuteronomy 27 and 28.

The reading ceremony was unique. With the Israelites in the valley (Shechem) between the two mountains, delegates from six tribes went to the top of Ebal, and representatives from the other six went to Gerizim. The curses were read from Ebal, no doubt a consequence of its condition and name, and the blessings were read from Gerizim. It would have been quite dramatic for the listeners below as these blessings and curses rang out across the valley. Through this dramatic enactment the message to Israel was clear: the choice of whether you'll be blessed or cursed is completely up to you.

What was not so clear was the picture of the cross and our redemption hidden in this event. Israel was commanded to build an altar on Ebal—none was built on Gerizim—on which they offered sacrifices and offerings to Jehovah. The barrenness and absence of life on Ebal represented us humans in our spiritually dead and cursed condition. The altar and sacrifices offered there symbolized Jesus' becoming our sacrifice in order to take our curse and spiritual death. He went to "Ebal," the place of barrenness and cursing, in order to give us the fruitfulness and blessings represented by Gerizim. The New Testament makes this clear:

> Christ redeemed us from the *curse* of the Law, having become a *curse* for us—for it is written, "*Cursed* is everyone who hangs on a tree"—in order that in Christ Jesus the *blessing* of Abraham might come to the Gentiles, so that we would receive the promise of the Spirit through faith.
>
> Galatians 3:13–14, italics mine

These verses make clear that because of Christ's sacrifice we have the awesome privilege of choosing the blessings of Deuteronomy 28. But there was another *part* of the ceremony that also pictured this great truth. Israel did more than sacrifice on Ebal's altar. They also whitewashed the stones and wrote on them all the words of the Law of Moses. This is detailed in Deuteronomy 27:1–8. Why this strange act? Not until the Holy Spirit interpreted it for us through the apostle Paul's writings do we see the answer:

> And you, being dead in your sins and the uncircumcision of your flesh, hath he quickened together with

him, having forgiven you all trespasses; blotting out the handwriting of ordinances that was against us, which was contrary to us, and took it out of the way, nailing it to his cross.

Colossians 2:13–14 KJV

Absolutely amazing.

I'm sure these Israelites on the mount of cursing didn't know they were painting a picture of the cross, where Christ would cancel the curses they were writing and bestow on us the blessings of redemption. It must have been quite a day for Christ as He watched this from heaven. Perhaps He winced a little as He watched the actions and listened to the curses being read from Ebal. The pain He would endure when fulfilling their prophetic actions would be horrific. And yet He must have smiled when He heard the wonderful blessings being read from Gerizim. "For the joy set before Him [Christ] endured the cross," the Hebrew writer told us (Hebrews 12:2).

Take some time and read Deuteronomy 27 and 28. Think of the price Jesus paid at the cross and determine to receive His blessings. In fact, why don't you declare the blessings mentioned in Deuteronomy 28 out loud over yourself and your family. Consider doing it daily for a while.

After this ceremony, the Samaritans built a temple on Gerizim, in opposition to the temple at Jerusalem. This became their place of worship. Though not sanctioned by God, it's easy to see why they chose Gerizim over Ebal as their place of worship. They problem is, we can't bypass Ebal (the cross) and go straight to the blessings. Many people try to do this. But there is simply no way home . . . without starting at the cross.

I encourage you to visit Ebal often in your meditations. You'll find on it an old rugged cross—worship Him there. The more you do, the more you'll find yourself at Gerizim.

> On a hill far away stood an old rugged cross,
> the emblem of suffering and shame;
> And I love that old cross where the dearest and
>   best
> For a world of lost sinners was slain.
>
> So I'll cherish the old rugged cross,
> Till my trophies at last I lay down;
> I will cling to the old rugged cross,
> And exchange it some day for a crown.[3]

Prayer

Father, I am so grateful for Your gift of grace—by it I am saved from eternal condemnation and empowered to live a life of victory. Jesus, it's Your cross that made that grace available, and today I choose to reflect upon and return to it.

Help me to truly find my way back to the cross, acknowledging and appreciating its significance. I am asking that You teach me to fully appropriate this heavenly endowment—cancelled curses and bestowed blessings of redemption. I know that receiving the full rights of sons is a choice left up to me.

I choose to live the chartered course of blessing laid out in Deuteronomy 28; diligently obeying Your commandments, Lord, and always walking in Your ways. May Your blessings pursue and overtake me such that I'll be favored everywhere I go. Blessed shall be all that I produce and touch, and victory over my enemies will be secured.

At the foot of the cross there is redemption; a fountain of blessing and abundant life. I choose to sit before the old rugged cross and drink deep as I enjoy the pleasure of Your company.

(Prayer taken from: Ephesians 2:5; Galatians 3:13–14; Galatians 4:5; 1 Peter 2:24; Romans 10:4; Acts 13:39; Colossians 2:13–14; Hebrews 12:2; Deuteronomy 28)

27

THE ADVANTAGE

I t is to your advantage that I leave," Jesus told His disciples (John 16:7). Can you imagine a more ridiculous-sounding statement? They had traveled with Him for three years, listening to Him expound on life, the ways of God, and the kingdom of heaven. His words carried such wisdom and authority that even His enemies said of Him, "Never has a man spoken the way this man speaks" (John 7:46).

They had watched Him cure blind eyes, open deaf ears, heal paralytics, cleanse lepers, and raise the dead. Once when He needed money, He procured it from the mouth of a fish. On another occasion, when He needed to cross a lake and didn't have a boat handy, He simply walked on water. And when storms tried to mess with

Him, He knocked the wind out of them with the power of His words.

Then He has the audacity to tell these men, "I'm going to leave you, and it's for your own good." One can only imagine the shock and disbelief of the disciples. It wasn't completely unheard of for Him to shock them with His statements. "You'll have to eat My body and drink My blood," He said to a large crowd on one occasion. Keep in mind these people didn't go to church every week and partake of Communion. They had no idea what He was talking about, and several of His followers left Him over it.

A short while before this preposterous "it's better for you that I leave" statement, Jesus was at it again, telling them things they wouldn't understand until later. This time He was waxing eloquent about heaven.

> In My Father's house are many dwelling places; if it were not so, I would have told you; for I go to prepare a place for you. If I go and prepare a place for you, I will come again and receive you to Myself, that where I am, there you may be also. And you know the way where I am going.
>
> John 14:2–4

At this point in His homily, Thomas—thank God for Thomas—spoke up and said what they were all thinking: "We don't have the slightest idea what you're talkin' about" (v. 5, Sheets' paraphrase). Jesus didn't seem too bothered by it and carried on with His speech.

Not understanding the "heavenly homes" statement was one thing; the disciples probably thought, "We'll just trust Him on that one." But this leaving business was different. Leaving? Better? I don't think so.

What *did* Christ mean when He said, "It is to your advantage that I go away"? Two understandings will help us. The first has to do with His choice of the word *advantage*, or as the King James Version says, "expedient." The Greek word is *sumphero*, which means "to bring together." Since bringing right things or people together produces benefits or an advantage, the word was used for the concept of expediency or gaining an advantage.

Christ was telling His disciples, "My departure will cause a new connection to take place for you. This 'bringing together' will be of great benefit to you, more so than even My physical presence."

The second piece of information that brings enlightenment to Christ's words is an awareness of who He was going to connect the disciples with: the Holy Spirit. Why would this relationship be so advantageous? Because He would be with them in spirit form, not in a flesh-and-blood body as Christ had been, and He could be everywhere at once. He could be "in" them, not just "with" them (John 14:17).

I don't believe many people come anywhere close to grasping this revelation in its fullness. God is in us. Yahweh, the Almighty, Everlasting God, the I AM—*that* God is inside us. What might we be like if we could only receive a full revelation of this? Perhaps we would become "little Christs," which is the meaning of the word *Christian*. Could it be that Christ's own words concerning us doing the same things He did would be fulfilled? Would we be miracle workers, life transformers, fearless, completely unselfish, and always led by the Holy Spirit? Would we walk in perfect love? As staggering as this seems, I believe we would.

Read what two leading Christian voices of our day wrote concerning the Holy Spirit. Jack Hayford says of Him:

- It is the Spirit who keeps the Word alive, and progressively being "incarnated" in me. . . .
- It is the Spirit who infuses prayer and praise with passion and begets vital faith for the supernatural.
- It is the Spirit who teaches and instructs me so that the "mirror" of the Word shines Jesus in and crowds sin out. . . .
- It is the Spirit who will bring love, graciousness, and a spirit of unity to my heart; so that I not only love the lost and want to see people brought to Christ, but I love all other Christians, and refuse to become an instrument of injury to Christ's body—the church.[1]

The late Bill Bright, founder of Campus Crusade for Christ, states it this way:

- He guides us (John 1:13), empowers us (Micah 3:8), and makes us holy (Romans 15:16). He bears witness in our lives (Romans 8:16), comforts us (John 14:16–26), gives us joy (Romans 14:17). . . .

- As our teacher of spiritual truths, the Holy Spirit illuminates our minds with insight into the mind of Christ (1 Corinthians 2:12–13) and reveals to us the hidden things of God (Isaiah 40:13–14). . . .
- As you are filled with the Holy Spirit, the Bible becomes alive, prayer becomes vital, your witness becomes effective, and obedience becomes a joy. Then, as a result of your obedience in these areas, your faith grows and you become more mature in your spiritual life.[2]

Great stuff. The Holy Spirit is all of this and more. He was Christ's helper and He must be ours, as well. As a human, Jesus was filled with, led by, empowered by, and anointed by the Holy Spirit (see Luke 4). Acts 10:38 also tells us Christ derived His power and anointing from the Holy Spirit. This very same Holy Spirit resides in us and wants to be our source of power and strength. But so often we don't make the connection, allowing His power to flow.

In a seminary missions class, Herbert Jackson told how, as a new missionary, he was assigned a car that would not start without a push. After pondering his problem, he devised a plan. He went to the school near his home, got permission to take some children out of class, and had them push his car off. As he made his rounds, he would either park on a hill or leave his car running. He used this ingenious procedure for two years.

Ill health forced the Jackson family to leave, and a new missionary came to that station. When Jackson proudly began to explain his arrangement for getting the car started, the new man began looking under the hood. Before the explanation was complete, the new missionary interrupted, "Why, Dr. Jackson, I believe the only trouble is this loose cable." He gave the cable a twist, stepped into the car, pushed the switch, and to Jackson's astonishment, the engine roared to life.

For two years needless trouble had become routine. The power was there all the time. Only a loose connection kept Jackson from putting the power to work.[3]

J. B. Phillips paraphrases Ephesians 1:19–20, "How tremendous is the power available to us who believe in God." When we make firm our connection with the Holy Spirit, His life and power flow through us. Don't waste this amazing help.

Second Corinthians 13:14 says, "The grace of the Lord Jesus Christ, and the love of God, and the fellowship of the Holy Spirit, be with you all." The term *fellowship* is from *koinonia* and is rich with meaning, revealing some of what the Holy Spirit wants to be in our lives. The following English words are all translations of *koinonia*:

- *Fellowship*—the Holy Spirit wants to visit with us.
- *Communion*—the Holy Spirit wants to commune with us.
- *Sharing together*—the Holy Spirit wants to share His insights and power with us.

- *Participation in or with*—the Holy Spirit wants to participate in our efforts and activities.
- *Distribution*—the Holy Spirit wants to distribute revelation, gifts, anointings, and blessings to us.
- *Impart*—the Holy Spirit wants to impart God's nature and benefits to us.
- *Partaking*—the Holy Spirit wants us to partake of His anointing and life.
- *Partnership*—the Holy Spirit wants to partner with us.
- *Companionship*—the Holy Spirit wants the pleasure of your company.

"May the *koinonia* of the Holy Spirit be with you." Wow. What a loaded statement. We are told in Proverbs that He wants an "intimate" relationship with us (3:32), not a superficial one. Psalm 25:14 says, "The secret of the Lord is for those who fear Him, and He will make them know His covenant." *Secret* and *intimate* are translated from the same Hebrew word *cowd,* which means "couch, cushion, or pillow." The picture is one of two intimate friends seated on a couch; or perhaps a wife and husband sharing a pillow, enjoying the pleasure of one another's company.

The Lord wants that kind of relationship with you—get to know Him!

Prayer

Thank You, God, that after Your Son Jesus' time on earth, You sent us another Helper—Yourself in Holy Spirit form—to dwell not just among but within us and to guide us as we steward the great victory that Jesus had won.

Holy Spirit, I long to experience all of who You are and what You do. I don't just want to know of You; I desire to have You alive and active in every part of my speech, actions, and thoughts. I want the Paraklete's *expediency and empowerment for Christ-likeness and kingdom advancement to be made manifest within me.*

Holy Spirit, You're the connection to sweet communion with the Father, further glimpses of God's depths, and doing greater works than Jesus did. Lord, help me to receive a full revelation of how I can be led of Your Spirit in every way. I lay open the Scriptures and position my heart to understand the koinonia *of the Holy Spirit. I request the pleasure of Your company.*

(Prayer taken from: John 14:16–26; John 1:12–13; Micah 3:8; Romans 15:16; Romans 8:16; 1 Corinthians 2:12–13; Isaiah 40:13–14; Luke 4; Acts 10:38; Ephesians 1:18–20; 2 Corinthians 13:14; Psalm 25:14)

28

THE FACE

This chapter is a little longer than the others but well worth the time.

When I was born my dad was a traveling evangelist. Those were the days when many evangelical churches had annual two-week revivals. The churches didn't pay much—sometimes Dad was actually paid with a few groceries, not money—which meant it was difficult for him to take time off. So he preached pretty much every night—on hellfire and brimstone. It worked, too. The preaching scared people to the "mourner's bench," the name used by many back then for the altar or kneeling bench. Dad could describe the fires of hell so well I would break out in a sweat.

Because of this I was saved at a very young age—several times, just in case! I think I may have been born again before I was even born! Because of this, a religious existence was all I knew growing up. A Christian was what I was and going to church was what I did. I heard so much about Scripture I was always one of the best in the Bible games we'd play at youth meetings, answering most trivia questions easily. I had a great biblical foundation, and when asked if I knew God, the answer was an immediate and unequivocal yes.

I didn't.

I knew who God was, and I was certainly born again. Nevertheless, I really didn't know Him in a personal way. I attended "God's house," as we referenced going to church, but I had never connected with His heart; tragically, I had known the promise of religion but never the pleasure of His company.

Being a born-again Christian doesn't equate to knowing God in a personal way. Growing up, I don't remember ever experiencing times with the Lord I would describe as intimate or heart-connections. I was not a hypocrite; I simply didn't know how to connect with God personally and at any real depth. In my family, being a Christian was just what we did. My dad was a preacher—I served my father's God. Period. Looking back, it's obvious that my mother was the greatest example of godliness in our home, but we maintained a very patriarchal culture, and therefore, Dad was the parent I looked to most as my example of a godly person.

When he quit the ministry, left home, divorced Mom, and married someone else, all of my worlds crashed: My family world was shattered, my religious world lost all credibility, and my personal world had a head-on collision with cynicism and rebellion. The two things that had brought me identity and stability—faith and family—were gone. Without these moorings I began drifting in the murky waters of pain, bitterness, and sin.

Looking back, I realize my personal faith simply wasn't strong enough to sustain me during this ordeal. I didn't know Yahweh experientially as *my* God; rather, He was my *father's* God. Consequently, when Dad failed and left me, so did his God. A secondhand, generation-removed God might get you to heaven, but He won't get you through much here on earth. When the going gets tough, He'd better be *your* God.

One of the great Hebrew patriarchs, Jacob, a grandson of Abraham, is a great biblical example of a "He's my father's God" kind of guy. His name, Jacob, means "heel-grabber," and one of its figurative meanings is "circumventing, as if by tripping the heels; also to restrain, as if holding by the heel." Jacob was given this name because he was born clutching the heel of his twin brother, Esau. The humorous aspect of his name, heel-grabber, became more than that for this Jacob. It was actually a play on words, prophetically picturing an evil side of this Jacob's nature, a conniving tendency toward holding back others in order to advance himself. The Amplified Bible uses four words to summarize what

Jacob became: *supplanter, schemer, trickster, swindler* (see Genesis 32:27). (For all of you actually named Jacob, take heart. The problem wasn't Jacob's name but his nature. Jacob is a name associated with honor and greatness in the eyes of God and men. Jehovah actually chose to call Himself "the God of Abraham, Isaac, and Jacob.")

It may surprise you to know that for the first forty or so years of Jacob's life, Jehovah was never even referred to as his God. He was referenced as "the God of Abraham and Isaac," never "the God of Jacob." His journey with the Lord began in Genesis 28, where Jehovah extended the same covenantal offer of blessing and partnership to Him He had originally made to Abraham.

> Then Jacob departed from Beersheba and went toward Haran. He came to a certain place and spent the night there, because the sun had set; and he took one of the stones of the place and put it under his head, and lay down in that place. He had a dream, and behold, a ladder was set on the earth with its top reaching to heaven; and behold, the angels of God were ascending and descending on it. And behold the Lord stood above it and said, "I am the Lord, the God of your father Abraham and the God of Isaac; the land on which you lie, I will give it to you and to your descendants. Your descendants will also be like the dust of the earth, and you will spread out to the west and to the east and to the north and to the south; and in you and in your

descendants shall all the families of the earth be blessed. Behold, I am with you and will keep you wherever you go, and will bring you back to this land; for I will not leave you until I have done what I have promised you." Then Jacob awoke from his sleep and said, "Surely the Lord is in this place, and I did not know it." He was afraid and said, "How awesome is this place! This is none other than the house of God, and this is the gate of heaven."

Genesis 28:10–17

Incredibly, after this dramatic dream encounter with the Lord, Jacob was still only willing to relate to Yahweh as Dad's and Grandpa's God, not his own. He actually told the Lord he still wasn't sure whether or not to make Him his God. He would decide later, *based on Jehovah's performance.*

Then Jacob made a vow, saying, "If God will be with me and will keep me on this journey that I take, and will give me food to eat and garments to wear, and I return to my father's house in safety, *then the* Lord *will be my God.*"

Genesis 28:20–21, italics mine

Can you imagine such audacity? "If you perform well enough, Jehovah—give me wealth, lands, protection, and favor—I'll choose you over Baal and the other gods of Canaan." Jacob clearly demonstrates that a Bethel ("God's house") experience, even receiving a powerful encounter with Him there, doesn't necessarily make Him your God.

To demonstrate that this was indeed the arrangement, six times over the next twenty years the Lord is referred to as the God of Jacob's fathers, but never is He called Jacob's God (see Genesis 28:13; 31:5, 29, 42, 53; 32:9). Godly parents, divine encounters, angelic visitations, supernatural dreams, and a visit to God's house weren't enough to transform Jacob's surface relationship with the Lord to one of the heart. They never are. Only intentional, personal decisions can transform the heart. I can't help but wonder how many Christians have been born again for five, ten, or even twenty years but like Jacob, and me in my early years, have never become intimately acquainted with God. Surface relationships abound in God's house. Deals are cut all the time: "You bless me and take me to heaven one day—I'll be a Christian."

What a tragedy.

This finally changed for Jacob two decades later after a second encounter with the Lord. This amazing meeting was so personal and powerful Jacob named the place *Penuel*, meaning "the face of God." Overwhelmed and changed, he declared, "I have seen God face to face" (Genesis 32:30). What a difference between Bethel and Penuel. Bethel, a "house of God" relationship, allows one to know the blessings of salvation without ever experiencing the pleasure of His company. At this level of relationship Jesus is more a Savior than a friend, and God is more of a distant ruler than an affectionate Father. A Penuel, face-to-face relationship, on the other hand, changes everything. Jesus becomes our Friend (John 15:15), God becomes Abba-Papa (Romans 8:15), and the Holy Spirit becomes our close Helper (John 14:16).

A deeper look at Penuel gives more insight. The term comes from *paneh*, the Hebrew word for "face." It is interesting and revealing that paneh is also the word for "presence." Turning the face toward someone, as in face-to-face encounters, obviously requires being in their presence. Thus, the word for "face" became the word for "presence." When the Scriptures speak of individuals having face-to-face relationships with God, or that God's face shines on us (Numbers 6:25; Psalm 80:3, 7, 19), they obviously aren't implying we're supposed to see His physical face. Rather, we're being reminded we can live in His presence, the intimacy of which is so personal it's akin to a face-to-face meeting with a friend.

The circumstances leading up to Penuel, the beginning of Jacob's face-to-face walk with God, are important to see, for they picture Yahweh's dealings with all of us on our journey from Bethel to Penuel. Jacob is about to go home, where he will face his brother, Esau, out of whom he had swindled the coveted firstborn birthright inheritance twenty years earlier. On the journey, Jacob moves ever closer to a confrontation with powerful Esau, who has heard of his approach and is on his way to meet Jacob with four hundred men. For Esau, revenge would be sweet.

True to form, conniving Jacob devises a plan to appease his still-offended brother, sending a series of gifts ahead. As he continues on his way, he ultimately sends everything he owns to Esau, including his servants. Eventually, he even sends his family. It must have been a painful sight as he watched them cross the stream called Jabbok, wondering if he would ever see them again (see Genesis 32:22).

Jabbok means "pouring out," and what an irony it is that this was the place where all of Jacob's accomplishments and wealth—his "house of God" blessings— were poured from him. God is determined to deepen the relationship and realizes that to do so He'll have to empty Jacob, at least temporarily, of all that matters more than Him.

What a scene this became. Jacob, who has spent his entire life conniving his way around and through every obstacle in his path, is wealthy—very wealthy—and has proven he is at the top of the food chain when it comes to manipulating circumstances.

Or so he thought.

God had an appointment scheduled with Jacob here at Jabbok, and in a day everything was gone, poured out to the brother he had swindled twenty years earlier. All in all, forty years of hard "heel-grabbing" were gone in a day.

The next verse sums up Jacob's circumstance and sets the stage for what is about to occur: "Then Jacob was left alone" (Genesis 32:24). Jacob has bought and connived his way out of trouble and into prosperity for the last time. He isn't yet aware of it, but Esau has become the least of his worries—he is alone with God, and this time it isn't for sweet dreams, as it was at Bethel! As preposterous as it sounds, Jacob and God will spend the night wrestling (see v. 24). That doesn't sound like fun!

The heavenly adversary begins by dislocating Jacob's thigh. In Scripture, a person's thigh represents his or her strength. Not only have Jacob's possessions and family been "poured out," God has now removed his strength. But there are not many people who could be as stubborn as Jacob. Still he fought.

"I won't let you go until you bless me," he says to his opponent, whom many scholars believe was an Old Testament, preincarnate appearance of Christ Himself. What is this blessing Jacob wants? Protection from Esau, of course. The Lord, however, is about to bless heel-grabber with something so much greater!

His initial response to Jacob's statement is so bizarre it almost sounds like a verse or two have been omitted. "What is your name?" He asks Jacob (Genesis 32:27). Try to picture this: two men fighting, one limping but holding on for dear life while demanding a blessing, and the other—who obviously knows His opponent—demanding to know his name. It could actually come across as humorous, if not ludicrous, if you didn't know what God was doing.

The Amplified Bible gives the clearest explanation I've seen or heard for this scenario. It translates Jacob's response in verse 27 this way: "And [in shock of realization, whispering] he said, Jacob [supplanter, schemer, trickster, swindler]!" Jacob was acknowledging his true nature: "I'm a conniving schemer."

Finally!

Jacob was pursuing one thing; God was after something altogether different. Jacob was seeking another blessing—protection; God was seeking Jacob. "It isn't your possessions, servants, or family I want, Jacob. [The Lord gave all of that back.] It's your old nature I'm after. You can con everyone else, but you can't con Me. I want you to realize, once and for all, that your strength is not what I need from you. I need for you to acknowledge your weakness—who you really are. Only then can I pour it out from you, delivering you from yourself. I want a far deeper relationship with you, one accessing your heart, not some 'deal' we cut involving temporal, earthly benefits. And since I'm God, by the way, I could kill you, but I'd rather just conquer your heart. Then we can run together and I can use you to help me save the world."

Amazing.

The fight was over the moment Jacob acknowledged his true condition. God's goal wasn't to win a fight but a friend. And what did He do next? Demonstrating His matchless grace, after changing this former heel-grabber's nature, He changed his name: "Your name shall no longer be Jacob, but Israel" (v. 28).

Don't misunderstand this. If Jacob is your name, you don't have to change it! The Lord continued referring to him as Jacob afterward. He was simply telling this particular Jacob that the negative symbolism the name had carried for him was gone. Now noble, patriarchal Jacob could emerge. In a matchless display of His grace, wisdom, and persistent love, God transformed this conniving swindler into a prince and patriarch, just as He intends to do with each of us. His sovereign actions made clear the bigger picture: "Now we can get on with the dream I gave you at Bethel, Jacob. Because the dream wasn't just for you; it was for Me, as well. And for the generations to follow! I told you I would bless all the nations of the world through you. I need a nation through whom I can demonstrate to the world My ways and heart, and through whom I can bring the Messiah. You're going to birth that nation for me, and you're going to do it from Penuel—my presence."

When God wrestled with Jacob, He was fighting for the heart of a man and warring for His dream of redeeming the human race!

Israel, leaving the fight with a life-altering limp, decided to name the place Penuel. Twenty years earlier Jacob entered Bethel, "the house of God," and found a dream. This day he had seen "the face of God" and found the Dream-Giver. He would never be the same.[1]

On the heels of this experience, there's one more scene too powerful to leave out. Jacob built an altar and gave it a name. In his day, altars were often monuments, a way of commemorating important events. In a sense they gave permanence to them. The name he gave the altar, El-Elohe-Israel (Genesis 33:20), was a magnificent statement. The phrase means "God, the God of Israel." Remember, Israel was not yet a nation; it was Jacob's new name given Him at Penuel. He was referring to himself. The monument was his declaration: "I've made my choice. Yahweh is not just my father's God—He's mine." I love it when a plan comes together!

A Bethel—"house of God"—relationship won't sustain you in the tough places of life. Just as important, it won't fulfill the portion of your heart created by God for the purpose of knowing and enjoying Him. You were made for Penuel—a face-to-face relationship with your Maker. Being a part of God's household, having a church home, or being in a family where God is served and honored is important and wonderful, but not enough. Sooner or later you'll need to graduate from His house to His face; from knowing Him as someone else's God to experiencing Him as your own. Only then will the promise of His company in heaven become the pleasure of His company here on earth.

Don't wait another day—find your Penuel.

Prayer

Father, I am grateful that I can meet with other Christians where we learn of You as Savior, Teacher, and Lord. But from there, I want to move toward the place called Penuel—the place where You and I meet face to face.

Jesus, deliver me from living in religion that would keep me stuck and satisfied with a partial, faulty view of who You are. I choose to empty myself of arrogance and self-sufficiency that would cause me not to seek out Your full heart. Holy Spirit, take me deeper, I want a greater revelation by experiencing Your presence. I want to know and be known by my God.

I don't ever want my life of Christianity to just be something that I do. I want to live it, breathe it, experience and protect it; zealously seeking to know Your heart and Your ways. I desire that my life of Christianity be lived enjoying the pleasure of Your company; conversing with my Best Friend and my Papa, face to face. Lord, cause Your face to shine upon me today.

(Prayer taken from: Genesis 32:30; 16:13; 1 Corinthians 13:12; Numbers 6:25; 12:8; Psalm 31:16; 80:3; 119:135; John 15:15; Amos 3:7; Galatians 4:6; Romans 8:15)

29

THE CONNECTION

Moses was dead (Joshua 1:2). It was bittersweet, for he was the last of a generation that had to die before the next generation was allowed to stop wandering in the desert and living in tents. Their inheritance awaited them—nice cities, homes, gardens, and more. After his death they could possess this inheritance. And yet Moses was the great leader that led them out of slavery with great signs and wonders. He knew God in ways no other mortal ever has. His staff parted waters, turned rocks into fountains, made the sky rain plagues and rivers turn to blood. He once spent so much time in God's glory that his skin glowed. Certainly this was no ordinary man.

But he was gone and his spiritual son, Joshua, was about to take over for him. He would lead this chosen nation into the Promised Land. For over four hundred years this had all been in the works. It started with Abraham, whom God chose to help Him redeem fallen humankind. Messiah would come through his offspring. As a thank-you, God promised him some land.

Abraham would have to wait for the land, however. Almighty God wouldn't simply take it from its current occupants and give it to him. In His justice, He would wait until the sins of the inhabitants reached a level that justified it (Genesis 15:16).

It was time.

What should be done to prepare for the momentous fulfillment of this great four-hundred-year-old promise? Four centuries is a long wait. Certainly something very special should be done over the next three days to celebrate and prepare. Should they fast for three days? Perhaps they should pray around the clock while they waited. Maybe they should worship nonstop for the next seventy-two hours. Should they offer hundreds, maybe thousands, of sacrifices? Or throw a three-day party? *Whatever we do, it needs to be monumental,* they probably thought.

When God's instructions came, there were two of them. The first was humorously practical. "Pack," He said. "Spend the next couple of days packing so you can cross the Jordan into your Promised Land" (Joshua 1:11, paraphrased).

Pack? Yep. Sometimes we want something that is simply profound, but God knows we need something profoundly simple. At times, the most spiritual thing we can do is the most natural and practical. Work is practical yet very spiritual; feeding hungry people is, as well; nurturing our children is practical, time-consuming, tiring—and very spiritual. Keepin' it simple is sometimes keepin' it spiritual. Movement requires preparation.

There was, however, another important assignment given in order to prepare for this historical day. It, too, would be simple, but would be an internal, not external, preparation. And it would be profoundly powerful and important. "*Qadash* yourselves," Joshua told them, "for tomorrow the Lord will do wonders among you," (Joshua 3:5). *Qadash* is an important Hebrew word meaning "to set apart." In biblical contexts, it usually meant "to be set apart *unto God*." There was another word for separation *from,* which we'll look at momentarily, but this one is *unto. Qadash* is often translated using theological words such as *sanctify* or *consecrate,* but don't let them confuse you. Keep it simple. The concept simply means "to separate or set apart a person or object unto God."

Setting a person or thing apart unto God meant it was reserved for Him. For example, furniture and utensils in the temple were *qadash*-ed to God, meaning they were not to be used for any other purpose. The Israelites were to be *qadash*-ed to God—they couldn't give themselves to the worship of other gods. I am *qadash*-ed to my wife, set apart to her alone.

On special occasions, the Israelites were often asked to *qadash* themselves to God in an extra special way.

This would be like Ceci and I getting away for a day or two, perhaps even for a vacation, in order to separate ourselves from other activities and spend extra quality time connecting with one another. Occasionally, God asked Israel to *qadash* themselves to Him in this additional manner.

The key to truly understanding God's heart in the use of *qadash* is the "unto Him" aspect. Though we have made sanctification and consecration religious and legalistic, they are actually relational concepts. A poor understanding of this has hindered our connection to Him. Consecration is for connection. In the same way that the wedding vow is relational, so is spiritual sanctification.

The Lord's request to Joshua and the Israelites before this monumental occasion was simple: "Draw near to Me today. Let's celebrate this new era by celebrating the pleasure of one another's company." How refreshing is that!

Interestingly, the Old Testament word for "holy," *qodesh*, comes from *qadash*. To be holy doesn't mean being separate "*from* sin," but rather "*unto* God." BIG difference. Inanimate objects were called "holy" in Scripture, as were places and days. Obviously, this was not because they hadn't sinned. It was due to the fact that they were being set apart to God. Holiness isn't sinlessness. Performing every good work imaginable would never make us *qodesh*—holy.

Please don't misunderstand me. To live a holy ("separated unto God") life will always result in purity, because connecting with God will make us like Him. His nature is imparted to us through the connection. *Qadash,* separation unto Him, is the cause; *qodesh,* holiness, is the effect.

There is another word in the Old Testament having to do with separation, but this one involves separation *from.* The word is *nazir.* You can probably see the word Nazirite in *nazir.* A Nazarite vow was a promise to separate from certain things, usually temporarily, as an outward demonstration of devotion to the Lord (see Numbers 1:2–21). It was a fast, of sorts.

Nazir, however, and Nazarite vows didn't make anyone holy. Only *qadash* led to *qodesh*—holiness. Can you see from these words and their definitions how backward we have this truth? Typically, we try to become holy through *nazir*—separation from doing certain things. "If I can only refrain from or stop this activity I can be holy," we tell ourselves. Then we make the effort to stay away from that sinful activity. When this approach alone is taken, however, there is no power flowing to us from His presence. If, on the other hand, our attempt at purity begins with *qadash*—separation unto the Lord—the connection provides the power and willpower necessary to overcome sin.

Samson is a good example of one who didn't get this right. He was supposed to be a Nazarite all of his life: separated from the dead, from unclean or forbidden foods, from alcohol, and from the cutting of his hair. These, however, were to be outward signs of his inward relationship with God. Samson obeyed the outward

Nazarite vow for part of his life, *nazir*-ing himself *from* those activities. But his Nazarite condition never made him holy. Try as you may, you'll never derive the word *qodesh* from *nazir*, only from *qadash*.

Sadly, there was never any indication that Samson was ever separated unto God. The inward pursuit never matched the outward vow. His hair was separated from a razor but his heart was never separated unto his God. Therefore, he yielded selfishness, lusts of the flesh, and compromise. Delilah and the cutting of his hair ultimately occurred because his heart connection had been cut off from God. Without power from this God connection, he was powerless against the temptation.

It is comforting to me that strength lies not in the perfection of my outward performance but the connection of my inward heart. I'd rather reach toward God than run from sin. I'll take a God who wants me over my good works any day.

A religious, legalistic approach to God leads to pride if we think we succeed, or hopelessness and condemnation if we fail. God hates pride and also dislikes hopelessness, knowing it leads to spiritual heart failure (see Proverbs 13:12). He wants our heart to be healthy through a connection with Him, the source of its life. There's a vast difference between performing *for* acceptance and performing *from* acceptance. God has already "accepted" us through Christ's sacrifice (Ephesians 1:6). Connect, celebrate His love and acceptance, and allow the power of His purity to flow through you.

Never again be satisfied with a performance-based, works-oriented relationship with God. His love isn't for sale—it cannot be earned. It is, however, available. Reach out to Him and receive it. Then, like Joshua and the Israelites, get ready to move into your glorious future, found in the pleasure of His company.

Prayer

Lord, help me to keep my Christianity real simple; resting in Your grace and trusting in Your love. Keep me from striving in my own strength toward perfection and feigning consecration through some fasts. You've only asked that I be set apart unto You.

I recognize that it's only from this special getaway place of relational exchange that I will receive the power and the will to walk in holiness and consecration; living a life truly set apart. I want to live a life of victory over sin and compromise, but on my own I know I'll quickly burn out.

Today I humbly draw near, God, and respond to the call to qadash myself unto You and away from other things. I need the power of purity that flows from Your presence; it's the heart connection by which I'm sustained.

Jesus, let me always be a burning, shining lamp, reflecting Your greatness and glory. For this I'll need Your nature imparted to me through time spent set apart in Your company.

(Prayer taken from: Joshua 3:5; Joshua 7:13; Proverbs 13:12; Revelation 2:7; Ephesians 1:5–6; John 15:1–11; 17:26; Numbers 1:2–21; John 5:35)

30

THE PRICE

You may have surmised by now that David, the great psalmist, giant slayer, and eventual king of Israel, is one my favorite Bible characters. I've written about him a good bit in this book. Jesus must have liked him, also; He accepted the title "Son of David."

David's ultimate success, in spite of his colossal failures, should bring hope to all of us. The "man after God's heart" also went after another man's wife, and the famous giant killer also caused the death of a loyal soldier—the woman's husband—in order to cover the affair. It doesn't get much worse than that. But forgiveness and cleansing are for sinners, not perfect people, and we all qualify. Someone once said, "The only perfect people are in heaven."

Indeed.

I thank God for His amazing grace. I love to sing the song and think often of its writer, John Newton, a former slave trader. It's hard for me to imagine a more despicable activity than slave trading. But truth and justice finally broke through the fog of deception, and after his conversion, Newton would eventually be a significant voice for the abolition of the slave trade. Later, he penned the famous words:

> Amazing grace, how sweet the sound,
> That saved a wretch like me.
> I once was lost, but now I'm found,
> Was blind, but now I see.[1]

Thank God for His amazing grace—and the song. Some historians actually believe Newton took the melody of "Amazing Grace" from the singing of slaves aboard one of his ships. Whether true or not, the irony that the song sang more than any other in the history of the world was written by a former slave trader is, like the song itself, amazing. But the song could not have carried us to such heights had not the man sank to such depths. And when all was said and done, the greatness of his sin was no match for the greatness of God's grace.

David would one day need—and find—this grace. But at the time when He became king, David was living a holy life of passion and purity, and he decided that his first order of business would be to move the ark of the covenant to Jerusalem. Over the ark was where God's presence and glory dwelled, and David, lover of God that he was, wanted this right next to the palace so he could make regular visits. He also wanted God's presence to be the focal point of the nation.

> Then David consulted with the captains of the thousands and the hundreds, even with every leader. David said to all the assembly of Israel, "If it seems good to you, and if it is from the Lord our God, let us send everywhere to our kinsmen who remain in all the land of Israel, also to the priests and Levites who are with them in their cities with pasture lands, that they may meet with us; and let us bring back the ark of our God to us, for we did not seek it in the days of Saul." Then all the assembly said that they would do so, for the thing was right in the eyes of all the people.
>
> So David assembled all Israel together, from the Shihor of Egypt even to the entrance of Hamath, to bring the ark of God from Kiriath-jearim. David and all Israel went up to Baalah, that is, to Kiriath-jearim, which belongs to Judah, to bring up from there the ark of God, the Lord who is enthroned above the cherubim, where His name is called. They carried the ark of God on a new cart from the house of Abinadab, and Uzza and Ahio drove the cart.
>
> 1 Chronicles 13:1–7

This was quite an undertaking. Samuel's version of the endeavor says David gathered thirty thousand specially chosen men of Israel to be a part of this procession (2 Samuel 6:1). Thirty thousand! He and the entourage were "celebrating before the Lord with all kinds of instruments made of fir wood, and lyres, harps, tambourines, castanets and cymbals" (v. 5). It must have been glorious.

Though David is about to make a serious mistake with the ark, give him credit. The ark and presence of God were important enough to him that He wanted this to be a BIG deal. "After all, this is Yahweh, God Almighty, we're talking about," was probably the reasoning. "Nothing is too much or too good for Him. In fact, make a new cart on which to transport it."

And that's where the problems started.

Because the ark was transported on a cart, pulled by oxen, it wasn't stable. When they hit a rough spot, the cart shifted and it looked like the ark might fall off. One of the drivers, Uzzah, touched it in order to steady it.

God killed him.

Talk about raining on a parade! The music and dancing stopped, as did the procession. Laughter turned to sorrow, and joy to mourning. A celebration became a funeral. David, uncertain of what to do, put the transporting of the ark on hold, housing it at the home of Obed-edom for three months while he researched what to do next.

The problem, David eventually discovered, was the mode of transportation—the new cart. The ark wasn't supposed to be transported in this manner but rather carried by poles running through rings on the sides of the ark. This way it was secure and didn't have to be touched. And though the process would be much more difficult, priests were supposed to carry the ark on their shoulders. The entire process was spelled out clearly in Numbers, the fourth chapter.

We are left to wonder what the motivation was behind David's using a cart. I believe it very likely boiled down to convenience. Carrying the ark on shoulders for ten miles would have been hard work. Splinters, sore muscles, chafed shoulders, blisters on the feet—all would have been the painful result. The long, hard miles up and down hills, across streams, in the heat—"let's just let the oxen do it." David learned the hard way that, contrary to human preference, ignorance *isn't* bliss, easy *doesn't* do it, and it's *not* just the thought that counts.

The three idiomatic expressions from which I took these statements may be witty, but often they're simply not true. In fact, they can be deadly. David and his followers discovered that it's more than the thought that counts. Obedience matters. And they learned that experiencing the Lord's presence and glory wouldn't be easy or convenient. As my friend Damon Thompson said recently, "If Christianity was intended to be convenient it wouldn't have been built on crosses and martyrs." God's presence and glory aren't stumbled onto by happenstance, nor are they found by the casual seeker. They're discovered when sought after, with passion and intentionality.

In *First Things First*, A. Roger Merrill tells of a business consultant who was moving into a new home.

He decided to hire a friend of his to landscape the grounds. She had a doctorate in horticulture and was extremely bright and knowledgeable.

. . . Because [the business consultant] was very busy and traveled a lot, he kept emphasizing to her the need to create his garden in a way that would require little or no maintenance on his part. He pointed out the absolute necessity of automatic sprinklers and other labor-saving devices. . . .

Finally, she stopped and said, "There's one thing you need to deal with before we go any further. If there's no gardener, there's no garden!"[2]

If there are no tired shoulders there will be no ark.

Our world has become obsessed with convenience. Whether it be our food, travel, communication, or gardens, we're determined to live "new cart" lifestyles. The trend has finally made it to church. We offer many convenient times, styles, and locations. Because we're so busy we even offer the condensed and abbreviated versions. Some congregations are now so efficiently convenient they can serve you your weekly God-connection in forty-five minutes, less time than it takes to watch your favorite television show: fifteen minutes of worship, fifteen minutes of announcements and fellowship, and a fifteen-minute message.

But wait, there's more. If that doesn't work for you, you can stay home and watch the service online. "And by the way, we promise not to mention anything that might convict or sadden you. There'll be no sin talked about, no grieving over the lost, and no mention of social and moral injustices such as abortion or human trafficking. We strive to make it quick, easy, and pleasant." I'm waiting for attendance "indulgences" to be sold: "Throw in an extra twenty bucks this Sunday and stay home with our blessing next week."

I don't believe our new-cart version of Christianity is God-honoring or biblical. The pleasure of His company is readily available, but it's not cheap. It will cost you time and effort. God wants intimacy with us, but He isn't an easy score. He expects marriage and covenant, not one-night stands. But I assure you, He is more than worth the price.

David and his leaders decided to give it another try—the inconvenient way. "Let's carry Him ourselves, on our shoulders and next to our hearts. It'll be hard work and will take all day, but having His presence and glory nearby will be worth it."

Now it was told King David, saying, "The Lord has blessed the house of Obed-edom and all that belongs to him, on account of the ark of God." David went and brought up the ark of God from the house of Obed-edom into the city of David with gladness. And so it was, that when the bearers of the ark of the Lord had gone six paces, he sacrificed an ox and a fatling. And David was dancing before the Lord with all his might, and David was wearing a linen ephod. So David and all the house of Israel were bringing up the ark of the Lord with shouting and the sound of the trumpet.

2 Samuel 6:12–15

In the Chronicles account of this, we're told that "God was helping the Levites who were carrying the ark of the covenant of the Lord" (1 Chronicles 15:26). Isn't that encouraging, and so typical of God's heart? When we honor Him by seeking His presence in the appropriate manner, He makes it easier to find Him. Our Father *wants* our company.

For David it had finally happened. The presence junkie would have unfettered access to the Lord and His glory. He placed the ark in a tent, called simply the "tent [or tabernacle] of David," and filled it with 24/7 worship. History tells us David himself spent hours at a time lingering inside. The inconvenience of the process had been rewarded with the enjoyment of His presence. Pursuit won.

This can be your story, as well. On this side of the cross our hearts are the tent. As unfathomable as it may seem, we are now the Holy of Holies. His presence is always with us and in us. You be the cart—that's what He really wants. Carry Him everywhere you go.

Reach for Him; He'll reach back. Make Christ your magnificent obsession, Yahweh your papa, and Holy Spirit your daily companion. Never again settle for the substandard existence of a life lived without *the pleasure of His company.*

Prayer

Father, You are worthy of the highest praise, the most extravagant adoration, and the furthest possible reaches of my love. Jesus, there is nothing I could ever give or do or say that will equate to the great sacrifice You've made. You've paid the price in full that we might have salvation, and yet, to freely bask in Your glory there is still a price that must be paid.

How can I bring to You an offering that costs me nothing? Father, I repent for doing this very same thing—trying to access the most exquisite of blessings while limiting You by what was easy or convenient. I confess to disobeying when You've called me to give more—a casual seeker so often I've remained.

More than the mere sacrifice of my lips, the sacrifice of my life is required that I might become an ark of Your glory and Your presence. Today, I purpose in my heart to give my time and effort toward fueling an intentional, passionate pursuit. Jesus, You are worth it all.

I refuse to live without experiencing the great pleasure of Your company, the depths of Your compassion, and the power of Your resurrection. Jesus, come be my magnificent obsession.

(Prayer taken from: 2 Samuel 6; 2 Samuel 24:24; Malachi 1:13–14; Romans 12:1; 1 Peter 2:5; 1 Chronicles 15:26; Luke 15:8; Proverbs 8:17; Hebrews 11:6)

NOTES

Chapter 1: The Person

1. Neil McAleer, *The Mind-Boggling Universe* (Garden City, NY: Doubleday & Company, 1987), n.p.

Chapter 4: The Dance

1. Adapted from Mark Littleton, *Escaping the Time Crunch* (Chicago: Moody Publishers, 1990), 238. Used by permission.

Chapter 5: The Search

1. Dutch Sheets, *Watchman Prayer* (Ventura, CA: Regal, 2000), 47.

Chapter 7: The Decision

1. Spiros Zodhiates, *Hebrew-Greek Key Word Study Bible: New American Standard* (Chattanooga, TN: AMG, 1990), 1729.

2. Adapted from Alice Collins, "All Those Years," in *Chicken Soup for the Mother's Soul*, ed. Jack Canfield, Mark Victor Hansen, Jennifer Read Hawthorne, and Marci Shimoff (Deerfield Beach, FL: Health Communications, Inc., 1997), 20.

Chapter 8: The Distractions

1. Jan Senn, "Carol Kent on Keeping Confident," *Today's Christian Woman*, January/February 1995, 68.
2. *The Consolidated Webster Encyclopedic Dictionary* (Chicago: Consolidated Book Publishers, 1954), s.vv. "disturb," "perturb," "turbulent."
3. Philip Yancey, "What Surprised Jesus," *Christianity Today*, September 12, 1994, 88. Used by permission.

Chapter 11: The Spoiler

1. Even though I believed in this person's gift very strongly, I also knew that no one hears from the Lord perfectly. That's why we are told to judge prophecy (1 Corinthians 14:29; 1 Thessalonians 5:19–21).

Chapter 15: The Friendship

1. Adapted from Dutch Sheets, *Dream* (Minneapolis: Bethany House, 2012), 101–106.
2. Haddon Robinson, "The Disciple's Prayer," *Preaching Today* no. 117, quoted in Greg Herrick, "Knowing God and Prayer," https://bible.org/book/export/html/6336.

Chapter 16: The Stretch

1. African folklore, as told by Dan Montano, "Lions or Gazelles?," *The Economist*, July 6, 1985, 37.

Chapter 17: The Undistracted

1. Tim Crothers, "The Face," *Sports Illustrated*, January 9, 1995, http://sportsillustrated.cnn.com/vault/article/magazine/MAG1006151/2/index.htm.
2. Edward K. Rowell, *Fresh Illustrations for Preaching and Teaching* (Grand Rapids: Baker Books, 1997), 93.

Chapter 18: The Courtship

1. Gordon Dahl, *Work, Play, and Worship in a Leisure-Oriented Society* (Minneapolis: Augsburg, 1972), 12.
2. Bil Keane, *The Family Circus*, King Features Syndicate comic strip, November 22, 1991.
3. This discussion on personally receiving God's revelation is adapted from Dutch Sheets, *The River of God* (Ventura, CA: Regal, 2000), 192–194. Used by permission.

4. Bob Greene, *Good Morning, Merry Sunshine* (New York: Penguin, 1985), 251.

Chapter 19: The Listener

1. T. H. White, *The Book of Merlyn* (Austin: University of Texas Press, 1977), ix–x.

Chapter 20: The Lingerers

1. Charles R. Swindoll, *Man to Man* (Grand Rapids: Zondervan, 1996), 272.

Chapter 21: The Visit

1. This chapter introduction originally appeared in Dutch Sheets, *Intercessory Prayer* (Ventura, CA: Regal, 1996), 159–160. Used by permission.

Chapter 22: The Prodigal

1. Adapted from S. D. Gordon, *What Will It Take to Change the World* (Grand Rapids: Baker, 1979), 17–21.

2. James Rowe, "Love Lifted Me," 1912 (lyrics in the public domain).

3. David C. Cooper, *Faith Under Fire* (Cleveland, TN: Pathway Press, 2001), 187.

Chapter 23: The Return

1. Bill Watterson, *Calvin and Hobbes*, Universal Press Syndicate comic strip, January 14, 1987.

2. William Cowper, "There Is a Fountain Filled With Blood," 1772 (lyrics in the public domain).

Chapter 26: The Altar

1. This chapter introduction originally appeared in Dutch Sheets, *The River of God* (Ventura, CA: Regal, 1998), 177–188. Used by permission.

2. Adapted from D. T. Forsythe, quoted in Roy B. Zuck, *The Speaker's Quote Book* (Grand Rapids: Kregel, 2009), 124.

3. George Bennard, "The Old Rugged Cross," 1912 (lyrics in the public domain).

Chapter 27: The Advantage

1. Jack W. Hayford, *The Power and Blessing: Celebrating the Disciplines of Spirit-Filled Living* (Colorado Springs: Victor Books, 1994), 21,

quoted in Robert Heidler, *Experiencing the Spirit* (Ventura, CA: Renew Books, 1998), 34.

2. Bill Bright, *The Holy Spirit* (San Bernardino, CA: Here's Life Publishers, 1980), 116, 121, quoted in Robert Heidler, *Experiencing the Spirit* (Ventura, CA: Renew Books, 1998), 35.

3. Craig Brian Larson, *Illustrations for Preaching and Teaching* (Grand Rapids: Baker Books, 1993), 182.

Chapter 28: The Face

1. Adapted from Dutch Sheets, *Dream* (Minneapolis: Bethany House, 2012), 146–148.

Chapter 30: The Price

1. John Newton, "Amazing Grace," 1779 (lyrics in the public domain).

2. Stephen R. Covey, A. Roger Merrill, Rebecca R. Merrill, *First Things First* (New York: Simon and Schuster, 1995), 77

Dutch Sheets is an internationally recognized author, teacher, and conference speaker. He travels extensively, empowering believers for passionate prayer and societal transformation. Dutch has pastored, taught in several colleges and seminaries, and served on the board of directors of numerous organizations. Seeing America experience a sweeping revival and return to its godly heritage is Dutch's greatest passion. He is a messenger of hope for America, encouraging believers to contend for awakening in our day and reformation in our lifetime.

Dutch has written more than twenty books, many of which have been translated into over thirty languages. His international bestseller, *Intercessory Prayer*, has sold over one million copies worldwide. Dutch's newest books, *The Pleasure of His Company* and *The Power of Hope*, were released in 2014.

Dutch and Ceci, his wife of more than thirty-five years treasure time spent with their two grown daughters, son-in-law, and grandchildren.

To learn more visit www.dutchsheets.org.

More From Dutch Sheets

To learn more about Dutch and his ministry,
visit dutchsheets.org.

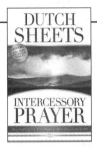

Discover your role as a prayer warrior—it can mean the difference between heaven and hell for someone you know! Armed with this book, you'll find the courage to pray for the "impossible" and the persistence to see your prayers to completion.

Intercessory Prayer

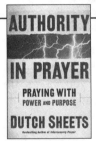

Don't allow sin, Satan, or the circumstances of life keep you from God's amazing promises! Learn how to pray with power and purpose, take hold of God's promises, and change your world through prayer.

Authority in Prayer

Your dreams and longings can reveal a lot about you—including God's true purpose for your life. Learn how to confidently know God's will and dare to turn your dreams into a soul-stirring partnership with God.

Dream

⬥BETHANYHOUSE

Stay up-to-date on your favorite books and authors with our free e-newsletters. Sign up today at bethanyhouse.com.

Find us on Facebook. facebook.com/BHPnonfiction

Follow us on Twitter. @bethany_house

More From Dutch Sheets

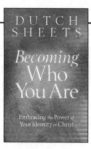

Revealing life-changing biblical truths about who you are in Christ, Dutch Sheets provides an action plan that will help you conquer whatever is keeping you defeated and enjoy newfound freedom.

Becoming Who You Are

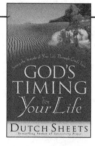

Offering fresh insight, Sheets uses Scripture to illuminate how the seasons in our lives are not unrelated, but rather different phases of a larger process. Through the stories of men and women throughout the Bible, you will see the ways in which God uses seasons of change to deepen our understanding of Him.

God's Timing for Your Life

Discover how to pray for the salvation of your friends and family in this practical book. You'll learn strategic biblical principles for this specific kind of intercession, and how to open windows of opportunity for the lost to be able to truly hear and receive the good news.

How to Pray for Lost Loved Ones

BETHANYHOUSE

Stay up-to-date on your favorite books and authors with our free e-newsletters. Sign up today at bethanyhouse.com.

Find us on Facebook. facebook.com/BHPnonfiction

Follow us on Twitter. @bethany_house